INSPIRED
DESTINY

Also by Dr. John F. Demartini

The Breakthrough Experience: *A Revolutionary New Approach to Personal Transformation*

Count Your Blessings: *The Healing Power of Gratitude and Love*

From Stress to Success . . . in Just 31 Days!

The Heart of Love: *How to Go Beyond Fantasy to Find True Relationship Fulfillment*

How to Make One Hell of a Profit and Still Get to Heaven

The Riches Within: *Your Seven Secret Treasures*

You Can Have an Amazing Life . . . in Just 60 Days!

All of the above are available at your local bookstore,
or may be ordered by visiting:

Hay House USA: **www.hayhouse.com®**
Hay House Australia: **www.hayhouse.com.au**
Hay House UK: **www.hayhouse.co.uk**
Hay House India: **www.hayhouse.co.in**

INSPIRED
DESTINY

Living a Fulfilling
and Purposeful Life

Dr. John F. Demartini

HAY HOUSE, INC.
Carlsbad, California • New York City
London • Sydney • New Delhi

Published in the United States by: Hay House, Inc.: www.hayhouse.com® • *Published in Australia by:* Hay House Australia Pty. Ltd.: www.hayhouse.com.au • *Published in the United Kingdom by:* Hay House UK, Ltd.: www.hayhouse.co.uk • *Published in India by:* Hay House Publishers India: www.hayhouse.co.in

Editorial supervision: Jill Kramer • *Project editor:* Lisa Mitchell
Design: Jami Goddess

The Demartini Method and The Breakthrough Experience are registered trademarks of Dr. John F. Demartini.

Library of Congress Cataloging-in-Publication Data

Demartini, John F.
  Inspired destiny : living a fulfilling and purposeful life / John F. Demartini. -- 1st ed.
      p. cm.
  ISBN 978-1-4019-2745-5 (tradepaper : alk. paper) 1. Self-help techniques. 2. Life skills. 3. Self-management (Psychology) I. Title.
  BF632.D46 2010
  158--dc22
                              2010002864

Tradepaper ISBN: 978-1-4019-2745-5
Digital ISBN: 978-1-4019-2862-9

1st edition, July 2010
1st digital printing, December 2016

Printed in the United States of America

For those individuals who have intuited their destiny:
an inspired, fulfilling, and purposeful life.

Since I believe that it is everyone's birthright to live in this way,
my intention for this book is to assist you in grabbing hold of the
abundant opportunities that surround you and help you fully live your
inspired destiny. May you now awaken to the truly amazing possibili-
ties before you. May you live an extraordinary life, and leave your
imprint and immortal legacy for generations or centuries to come.

CONTENTS

PART III: Life Insights

FOREWORD

*When you see genius in others, you
have the power to awaken them to it.*

Many people have heard and been inspired by Dr. John Demartini's story, yet few comprehend its true significance as it relates to their *own* lives and the possibilities that are inherent in the human spirit.

So often when we meet those whom we perceive to be successful, we assess them only in the present moment. In other words, we either don't know or dismiss the details relating to the focused effort exerted over time to realize a particular goal or level of success. We may polarize our perceptions by putting these successful individuals on a pedestal and justifying their achievements by thinking that they're the "lucky ones." Thus, we minimize our own accomplishments by believing that we're among the "less fortunate." Dr. Demartini's life story—if we really pay attention—turns the paradigm of current thought into a new realization. We can see what's possible for *our* lives when we find something that truly inspires us beyond the limitations of our own beliefs about ourselves.

At the age of 17, John Demartini still struggled to read and had completely bought into the idea that he was learning disabled with no chance of doing anything significant or meaningful with his life. His vision was to be a surfer, yet it extended no further than the scope of surfing daily, board making, and "recreation."

However, one event, one man, changed his life forever, awakening a new vision that empowered him to conquer his reading, learning, and speaking challenges. Today, this vision defines him as a human behavioral specialist, a profound educator dedicated to expanding human awareness and potential across the planet.

His story is every person's story. We minimize ourselves when we think that it's something outside of us that determines our destiny. We aren't limited by where we come from, what we have, or what we haven't experienced. Not by our education or our lack of it. Nor by our financial status or our upbringing. Neither do the opportunities or people or places we've encountered define our future success and fulfillment. What determines our destiny is our ability to clarify what's most inspiring to us—something so inspiring that we're willing to dedicate our lives to building it. The magic ingredient to success is hard work, and we won't endure the hours it takes to reach our goals unless that work ties to our true inspiration. Dr. Demartini puts in the hours—but as he would say, when we do what we love and love what we do, time flies and energy abounds.

We all deserve to know the truth of our potential and have the tools to activate and empower our lives. This book is about Dr. Demartini doing for *you* what someone else did for him many years ago. It's a book about helping you awaken your inspiring vision so that you have your own heartfelt dream to work on throughout your life.

Inspired Destiny will teach you about human behavior: why you are who you are; what drives your inspiration; how you are perfect just as you are; and how both your strengths and weaknesses, and supports and challenges, create the perfect dynamic to assist you in doing what you most love right now and also what you'd most love to do in the future. This book can be aptly summed up as a handbook for life, as it contains all the wisdom you need to understand the essence of who you are, as well as the know-how to empower all aspects of your life.

At its center, this book has a truly inspired heart, and I know that it will touch and transform the lives of many people across the world. May you be such a person so that you get to set in motion what you intend, and discover all that you can create, with the time and talents you have been given.

— **Clarissa Judd**
Director of the Demartini Institute
South Africa

INTRODUCTION

The book you're holding in your hands emerged out of a program (also called "Inspired Destiny") that I've been presenting in South Africa. This powerful one-day event assists young adults in discovering their life purpose and overcoming adversity to pursue just that: an inspired destiny. Although born from this initial cause, this project evolved into a deeply meaningful book containing practical tools that can be used by people of all ages.

If you seek greater significance and purpose in your life, you've come to the right place. Whether you're a young adult or simply young at heart, I will provide the direction and guidance to catalyze your inspired destiny.

"Part I: Values, Purpose, and Destiny" provides a comprehensive introduction to human behavior, giving you the tools and insights to discover what's truly important to you, and how this relates to realizing your purpose. You'll learn how to clarify what you'd love to dedicate your life to, communicate your goals powerfully and effectively to others, make money doing what you love, and explore many myths and principles that will empower you on the journey to living a fulfilling life.

"Part II: Life Skills" equips you with some of the most powerful tools for identifying and overcoming the greatest challenges you face on the path to your inspired destiny. You'll learn how to dissolve the emotions that can distract you from your purpose, including fear of the future, guilt about the past, resentment, regret, depression, intimidation, stress, grief, loss, and betrayal. You will then have the tools to overcome obstacles and plan your life the way you would truly love it to be.

"Part III: Life Insights" holds many keys to mastering and living a meaningful, inspiring life. You will explore the power of living with an astronomical vision, find out the differences between leaders and followers, uncover the five S's of leadership, and expand your time horizons; as well as understand the nature of the ripple effect and learn ways to set an example for others by doing what you love.

Throughout *Inspired Destiny*, there are powerful exercises ("Get Inspired!") to help you break through your fears and obstacles so you can become clear about what you'd love to dedicate your life to. I recommend that you complete these exercises as you go. At the end of each chapter, I've also included a summary of what you've just read, called "Inspired Insights," immediately followed by "Words of Power," which are affirmations you can use to take these principles and practices off the page and into your life. You deserve a fulfilling and meaningful life, and these tools will set you free to do just that.

Congratulations on following your intuition and reasoning by picking up *Inspired Destiny*—and on pursuing a life of greatness.

PART I

VALUES, PURPOSE, AND DESTINY

CHAPTER 1

Your Life Can Be Inspiring

"The meaning of life is to give life meaning."
— **Ken Hudgins**

If you're like millions of people worldwide, you may be asking yourself why you're here and what you want to do with the time you've been given. *What would I love to do with the rest of my life? What meaningful purpose shall I dedicate myself to? Toward what chief aim shall I direct my future?*

Figuring out what you'd love to do every day can be one of the most challenging, yet inspiring, tasks you'll ever undertake. If and when you get clear on your life's direction, you may then face many obstacles along the path to fulfilling your purpose, goals, or dreams. But these challenges will define who you are and who you can become. They will also help you refine your answers to the questions above.

Yes, life can be difficult at times—indeed, some of history's greatest minds and achievers have faced incredible obstacles but went on to leave their mark by doing something truly significant and inspiring. Think of Albert Einstein, a genius in physics who was supposedly bad at math. Or Michael Jordan, who was cut from his high-school basketball team but went on to redefine the sport.

Or Abraham Lincoln, who was born into poverty, whose mother died young, and who was faced with defeat repeatedly but went on to become one of the greatest U.S. Presidents in history. Consider any of the thousands, perhaps millions, of other individuals who started out with seemingly insurmountable barriers but ultimately accomplished what many now admire.

What makes people like this stand out? Well, they go after their dreams with everything they've got and everything they've been given. *You can, too!*

Buried in your heart is a powerful knowing. It holds the secrets to what you'd love to spend your life doing and a dream of how you'd love to make an impact on the world. In every moment, your experiences reveal your purpose and guide you to recognize it for yourself. Ultimately, your purpose revolves around what you perceive to be most important, and your inspired destiny resides in the essence of what you believe to be truly valuable and meaningful.

In the next several pages, I'd like to share parts of my life story and how I was able to tap into my true purpose. I've talked about these early experiences in some of my previous books, but I feel that it's necessary to repeat them here because they're authentic and illustrate that in spite of setbacks, disabilities, or any other limitations or obstacles, it's possible for you to discover your destiny and live each day in an inspired and meaningful way.

When I was seven years old, my first-grade teacher told me that I'd never read, write, or communicate properly. She doubted that I'd ever amount to anything or go very far in life. With my learning difficulties and a diagnosis of dyslexia, I must have shown little promise. But I made it through elementary school by asking the smartest students in the class what they got out of each subject and book. By that point, I was already trying to overcome my teacher's challenging prediction.

Not long afterward, my parents moved us from the large city of Houston, Texas, to a small town in the country, where the nearest neighbor was a mile away. Many of the children attending the local school were rough: on my first day, I was beaten up and left with a black eye and busted nose. The population of the area was at a low socioeconomic level, and education wasn't high on the cultural-values list, so I didn't have a team of smart boys and girls who could answer my questions about the classes. I soon started failing.

My parents could see that I wasn't going to make it in school because of my learning difficulties, so they, like my first-grade teacher, encouraged me to pursue my love of sports instead. Although initially I was focused on playing baseball and wanted to play professionally someday, after moving to this small town, my aspirations quickly faded. Kids in gangs and opposing team members would attack me when I pitched and won, so I left the baseball field for good.

Still, I had another dream: to surf big waves. With my parents' blessing, at the age of 14, I decided to leave school and hitchhike to California, then eventually fly off to Hawaii. My father made sure that I had a minimum of $13 with me, telling me never to carry less than that or I could be jailed for vagrancy. My mother even had a document notarized that basically stated: "My son isn't a runaway. He's a young boy with a dream." It looked like this:

AFFIDAVIT TO ANY FACT
THE STATE OF TEXAS,
COUNTY OF FORT BEND

BEFORE ME, THE UNDERSIGNED, a Notary Public in and for said County, State of Texas, on this day personally appeared Mrs. Adolph G. Demartini, mother, to me well known to be a credible person, and who, after being by me duly sworn, on her oath stated:

That the affiant is the mother and legal guardian of John Frederic Demartini, John is fourteen (14) years of age, and resides with his family at Route 2, Box 34, Richmond, Texas 77469.

John departed with the affiant's blessings, permission, and best wishes for an enjoyable visit to California, the thirty-first (31st) State of the United States of America. The affiant further states that neither John nor any member of the families to whom John is related has any living relations residing in the State of California.

_____

Beth T. Demartini
Mrs. A. G. Demartini

SUBSCRIBED AND SWORN TO BEFORE ME, this 10th day of June, A.D. 1968

_____

Notary Public in and for Fort Bend County, Texas

My parents dropped me off by the freeway (Interstate 10) and wished me well. "Go and live your dream, son, because you're torturing yourself trying to be somebody you're not."

That's a pretty amazing thing for parents to do: that is, allow their barely teenaged son (who clearly wasn't going to make it academically) to hitchhike out of state in order to live his dream of surfing big waves. Yet I was mature for my age, and my parents had given me many responsibilities to help me grow in other ways.

The Wisdom of Love and the Love of Wisdom

Making my way to El Paso, about halfway to California, I met a man who started walking with me, and he asked if I was a runaway.

"No, I'm not. My parents gave me a ride to the freeway," I explained. Maybe he had run away himself a long time ago. He looked like someone who lived on the streets.

The man inquired whether I was going to California, and when I told him that I was, and why, he led me to a corner malt shop and bought me a Coca-Cola. As I finished my drink, he looked at me intently.

"There are two things I want to teach you, young man. You have to promise you'll never forget them."

After I agreed, we walked a couple of blocks to the downtown El Paso library. Leaving my surfboard at the entrance, I sat down at a table inside while the man retrieved a couple of books.

He set them on the table next to me. "First, don't ever judge a book by its cover. It will fool you."

"Yes, sir." I'd heard that before.

"You probably think I'm a bum." He was right; I did. The fellow looked the part, being unshaven and dressed in somewhat unkempt clothes.

"Young man, I am one of the wealthiest people in the world," he continued. "I have everything money can buy: ships, planes, cars, homes, and so forth. About a year ago, someone very special to me passed away. I reflected on my life and realized that my time is going to come, too. I thought about how fortunate I had been and realized that the only thing I didn't possess was the experience of what it was like to have nothing. I decided to take a year off so that I could make my way across America and find out what it's like to be without. So let me repeat this: don't ever judge a book by its cover."

Then he reached over and placed my right hand on the two books he'd set on the table; one was by Plato and the other was by Aristotle. The man said, "Second, I want you to learn how to read, boy. There are only two things in this world that can never be taken from you, and those are your love and your wisdom. They can take away your money or your family, but they can never take away your love and wisdom. So you must learn how to read in order to gain the wisdom of love and the love of wisdom. Don't ever forget that."

Afterward, the man returned the books to their shelves and walked me outside the library, leading me to where I could continue on my way to California.

Although I didn't get the significance of this encounter at the time, today my life is dedicated to the very thing this man championed: the love of wisdom and the wisdom of love.

A Near-Death Experience

After I made it to California, I panhandled to survive. I went into diners and took leftover food off tables, lived behind buildings near vents to keep warm at night, and did all of the things you do if you're a teenager living on the streets. As soon as I had enough money, I bought a ticket to fly from California to Hawaii. By then, it was the junction of the late 1960s and early 1970s, and I began surfing on the North Shore of Oahu. I was in the ocean every day, and was also trying to expand my consciousness—I'm sure you understand what I mean by that—with organic, natural herbs and mushrooms.

When I first got to Hawaii, I lived underneath a bridge before moving to Ehukai Beach Park and sleeping under a park bench. After it rained on me, though, I moved to a public bathroom, and then got lucky when I found an abandoned car for my new home. Finally, I got a tent and set up my little abode in a jungle close to the beach near Haleiwa.

While I was staying there, I ate the seeds from the Hawaiian Baby Woodrose, a plant that contains a compound that makes everything look colorful. The seeds were covered by a coat of fuzz that's made up of a chemical much like strychnine, which damages the neuromuscular system. After months of consuming the seeds, I began to get cramps all through my body. My fingers and toes started locking up, but at the time, I attributed it to my surfing 11 hours a day. I started eating bananas and drinking grapefruit juice hoping that the potassium would reduce the cramps, but it didn't help. One day I was surfing 30-foot-face waves when the entire right side of my body constricted, and my diaphragm was paralyzed.

I almost died in the water, but eventually I came to the surface and got my breath back. I made it back to shore, but I was all cut up and my board was completely destroyed. I somehow managed to stumble off the beach and into the nearest supermarket with a strong craving for buttermilk, which I'd never had before in my life. I drank it, walked to the parking lot, and passed out.

To this day, I have no idea how I got back to my tent. I lay there semiconscious for three and a half days before someone found me, dehydrated, severely ill, and nearly dead. A kind lady who'd been walking through a nearby jungle path and heard me in distress helped me recover and clean up. Then she took me to a health-food store called Vim & Vigor and bought me a carrot-juice drink to settle my stomach.

There in the store, a guy with a huge blond Afro took one look at me and said, "Man, you need to take a yoga class—your body is screwed up."

A few days later when I walked out of that same health-food store, I saw a flyer on the door:

SUNSET RECREATIONAL HALL
SPECIAL GUEST SPEAKER PAUL C. BRAGG
YOGA CLASS

Because one of the words on the flyer was *yoga,* I intuitively decided I should go.

Discovering My Purpose in Life

There were about 35 people sitting on a wooden floor as a yoga instructor introduced Paul C. Bragg, an elderly white-haired wise man, the founder of American health-food stores, and a legend due to his impact on the health-food industry around the world. Paul had almost died as a teenager, but when I met him, he was working toward his first century of life. He'd dedicated himself—since the age of 15—to maximizing human longevity and potential. When he spoke, people listened. He had wisdom that far exceeded anyone else in the room.

Everyone has a body, mind, and soul, Paul told us. The body must be guided by the mind, and the mind must be guided by the soul to fully realize our potential. Inside all of us is a yearning to do something amazing and magnificent—something profound, inspiring, and reflecting true leadership.

His words were a revelation to me. Never before had I met someone who was so inspired and present, so intently focused, and who so clearly loved what he was doing. You could hear a pin drop in the room that evening, as everyone was paying rapt attention.

Paul spoke for about 45 minutes and then announced that this was a special occasion: "Tonight I'm going to give you ten minutes to think about what you want to dedicate your life to. Whatever you decide during this exercise will become your destiny."

Now *that* was a heavy-duty task to ask of an almost 18-year-old guy! Before that night, I'd just assumed that I'd make surfboards on the North Shore of Oahu for the rest of my life. I was going to live in my tent for as long as I could, at least until I got kicked out and had to go somewhere else. Those were my ambitions.

But something happened in that moment. Paul Bragg, vibrantly alive and inspired, sparked a new possibility for me as I sat there on the floor, reviewing my life. I saw myself in leg braces as a kid, correcting a birth defect that I had . . . then in the first grade, being diagnosed as a learning-disabled dyslexic who was told that I would never amount to anything or go far in life . . . then hitchhiking through El Paso and meeting the "bum" who shared his love of wisdom and the wisdom of love . . . then in my tent almost dead. Finally, I saw myself in the present moment, looking up at Paul Bragg, a visionary making a difference in people's lives around the world by fulfilling his purpose.

Wow—I would love to be able to do for others what this man has just done for me! I decided right then to study and adhere to Paul's teachings, which he'd introduced as Universal Laws that related to the body, mind, and spirit. (First and foremost, I knew I needed to focus on the physical to deal with the toxicity and spasms still racking my body.)

I declared to myself: *I am going to become a teacher, healer, and philosopher. I will find a way to travel the world and set foot upon every country across the face of the earth, share my research with others, and help everyone live inspired and magnificent lives.* Who knows where that came from (and, at the time, it wasn't stated so eloquently), but that's what came to me that night. Paul then conducted a guided visualization/meditation, and I was able to form a crystal clear vision of myself standing on a balcony before a crowd of a million people, sharing and speaking. That vision was so strong and inspiring that I was brought to tears.

After 15 minutes of meditation, I opened my eyes and looked around the room. All of the other participants were deeply moved, too; everyone was inspired and in tears. Every single person had seen a vision of what he or she would love to do in life. I gazed

11

over at Paul, who was sitting with his eyes still closed and his hands on his knees. You could almost read his mind. It was as if he were saying: "Thank You, God, for revealing the destinies of these young souls."

Yes, *destiny*. I saw a clear vision of how all my experiences were pointing me toward a path I'd never known existed. There were no mistakes. Everything I'd experienced was directing me to do something truly extraordinary with my life. Today, I've worked with millions of people, and I'm certain that this is a great truth that applies to everyone: **All of the events and circumstances in your life mold you, refine you, and guide you to discovering and fulfilling your most meaningful purpose.** What you experience reveals your destiny to you in every moment.

Certainty at Fort DeRussy

Eager for more of what Paul Bragg had to offer, the next morning I hitchhiked to the first of a series of daily classes that continued for three weeks, which Paul was offering at Fort DeRussy on the other side of the island. When I arrived, I noticed that there were 50-, 60-, and 70-year-old people in his class. All of us went on a jog together around the nearby park, doing our best to keep up with Paul! When we came back, we consumed water and fruit while our leader lectured us on the Laws of the Universe and health for 45 minutes.

For the next 21 days, I studied with Paul every morning. He taught us about the power of visualization, thoughts, and affirmations. He spoke about what he called the "seven doctors of natural healing" and shared the principle and effectiveness of what later become known as the "Law of Attraction."

At the end of the three weeks, Paul bid us farewell: "I love you all. I'm going back to Mount Shasta in California, and I hope to see you again someday."

My heart sank. My mentor was leaving me alone with my newly discovered dream of being a teacher, healer, and philosopher.

When he was around, I felt like I was making progress. Without his guidance, though, I had no idea what I was going to do. I waited until everyone left and then approached him.

"Mr. Bragg, I'm John Demartini. I attended your evening presentation three weeks ago."

"Yes, John, I remember."

"You said that whatever we decided that night would be our destiny. Well, I saw that I would be a great teacher, healer, and philosopher; I saw myself traveling the world, stepping foot in every country, and sharing my research . . . but I've never read a book from cover to cover in my life. How will I achieve what I imagined?"

"Is that it? You don't read? Are there any other problems?"

I shook my head. "No, sir, that's my problem."

He gave me a serious look. "That is not a problem, John. Every day for the rest of your life, I want you to say this to yourself: *I am a genius, and I apply my wisdom.*"

I tried the words out. "I am a genius, and I apply my wisdom?"

"Yes, that's right."

I said it over and over again. Paul Bragg had me repeat it with my eyes closed until I really felt it. Then he patted me on the shoulder and instructed me to persist.

"Never miss a day for the rest of your life. Say it every day and soon your cells will tingle with it, and so will the world."

Since then, for nearly 40 years now, I've recited that one affirmation every single day of my life.

My Onward Journey

When I got back to the North Shore, I found my buddies expanding their consciousness through natural herbal means. I opened the flap of my tent and said, "Hey, guys, guess what?! I'm a genius, and I apply my wisdom!"

They all laughed, rolling around on the floor. "John is a genius! Woo-hoo!"

Right then I realized that you don't need to tell everyone about your dreams. When you discover your purpose in life and then share it with others who have smaller visions, they might try to bring you back down to the size or magnitude of their own goals. But if you tell your dreams to people who have even greater ambitions than you, they'll encourage you to go for it and to set the bar even higher.

With that in mind, I decided to start doing what Paul Bragg had recommended. I fasted for a while to reduce the effects of my toxic poisoning, and then ate healthy, nutritious foods. I also began meditating; and during one session, I heard an inner, intuitive message that it was time for me to leave Hawaii and go back home to see my parents. Shortly afterward, I flew to California and hitchhiked to Houston.

I hadn't been home long when my mother suggested that I take the General Educational Development test, or GED (a high-school-equivalency exam), which I somehow passed by guessing and filling in the dots on the page while repeatedly affirming: *I am a genius, and I apply my wisdom.* Then my mom said that since I'd had such good luck with the first test, I should take the college entrance exam. Maybe I'd pass that one, too—and indeed, I did.

So I enrolled in my first college courses . . . *me,* the dyslexic surf bum who had nearly died alone in a tent. The dramatic change was exhilarating, but I soon came up against my previous limits and nearly failed one of my classes. This just made me more determined to overcome my dyslexia, so I decided to read the dictionary from front to back, which would also expand my vocabulary, and then I would move on to encyclopedias. With that discipline and my undeterred determination, my reading and writing steadily improved, and I gradually began doing well in school.

Two years after Paul Bragg had shared that affirmation with me, I was in a college library, tutoring 15 to 20 other students in mathematics. Gathered around a large table, we were working on a calculus problem, and I overheard one student say to another, "That Demartini is a friggin' genius."

The remark startled me, but only because I hadn't heard anyone else say it before; of course, I'd recited it hundreds of times in my own mind. Now, the realization that my destiny was at hand brought tears to my eyes as I remembered what Paul had told me: "What you see for yourself, what you say to yourself, how you feel about yourself, and what actions you do for yourself will determine your destiny."

He was right. Since then, I've gradually developed speed-reading skills and have read nearly 29,000 books in more than 275 different disciplines regarding the Laws of the Universe. Today, I travel full-time, sharing my research findings and teaching millions of people around the world how to live an amazing life by fulfilling their inspired destiny.

Discovering Your Purpose Early On

There's no law that says you can't discover your purpose at an early age. Some people decide to become skateboarders, teachers, dancers, and performers when they're young; and they go on to do just that. When I lived on the North Shore, I used to watch the now famous surfer Laird Hamilton. Just seven or eight years old at the time, he'd play on the beach, running around and jumping onto flat boards, and learning to surf pipeline. Laird knew when he was just four years old that he wanted to be a great surfer and ride the biggest waves. Today, he's one of the biggest wave riders in the world because he found his niche early on and dedicated his life to achieving that dream.

He's not the only one. Once when I was flying from Houston to New York I spotted a lady sprinting through the airport while wearing sunglasses, which seemed a little odd. Was she supposed to be incognito or something? She boarded the plane last with me (I was late, too). About 30 minutes after takeoff, I walked to the restroom in the back of the plane, where I noticed the woman sitting in the last row, still wearing her sunglasses. Maybe she was on drugs, or perhaps she was a movie star. There was definitely something different about her.

As I was waiting in line, I motioned to her sunglasses and looked at her quizzically. At first she ignored me, so I sat down in the vacant seat next to her and asked what she did for a living. After questioning me and satisfying herself that I wasn't a reporter, she revealed that she was an actress and had been in *Blazing Saddles* and a few other films.

As we chatted, I asked her how she got into the business. It turned out that when she was three years old, she'd watched Judy Garland on TV performing a song-and-dance routine. In that moment, she knew that she wanted to be onstage. (I wonder if she knew that her inspiration, Ms. Garland, also realized her calling when she was about the same age.) So my mysterious friend had taken classes in singing and dancing and had talked her parents into allowing her to do whatever it took for her to realize her dream. She later became an accomplished actress, singer, and dancer. She had an advantage because she'd decided on her purpose very young, whereas some people meander through life without finding out what they'd truly love to do.

Discovering your purpose is essential for living a fulfilling and meaningful life, so why not do it now? There's nothing wrong with being unclear about what's in your future, but my experience says that somewhere inside, you already know what you'd love to do. There may be anxieties or fears that block you from admitting or revealing it to yourself, but your magnificent cause does lie deep within.

No matter who you are, where you've been, where you come from, what you've been through, or what your beliefs about yourself or your life are, it's possible for you to discover what you'd love to do—and overcome any challenges to fulfill your destiny. Whatever your dream is, you can achieve it.

Inspired Insights

- Buried in your heart is a powerful knowing, telling you what you'd love to dedicate your life to.

- Your purpose is built on what you perceive to be most important to you.

- Your life's challenges and experiences are directing and guiding you to do something truly magnificent with your life.

- Discovering your purpose as early as possible gives you an advantage in building momentum, achieving your dreams, and revealing your inspired destiny to the world.

Words of Power

Choose at least one of the following affirmations and repeat it to yourself every day for at least the next month (ideally for the next few months). If this seems particularly challenging (or particularly rewarding), make a commitment to repeat it to yourself every day for the rest of your life.

I know what I would love to do, and I pursue it.

My life reveals my purpose in every moment.

I know my inspired destiny, and I take action toward fulfilling it.

*My challenges direct me to do something
truly magnificent with my life.*

CHAPTER 2

What Is "Missing" in Your Life?

"There is nothing absent or lacking.
Everything is present, already in potential."
— **Lopon Tenzin Namdak**

Everyone lives by a set of priorities, a "hierarchy of values" determined by conscious or unconscious "voids"—that is, something that is perceived to be missing or unfulfilled. A void may be a burning question you want to answer, a mystery you wish to solve, or a challenge you'd love to overcome. Whatever you believe is most missing in your life becomes most *important* and therefore most *valuable* to you. You spend the most time, money, and energy on your *highest values*.

For example, if you perceive yourself as lacking a romantic relationship (and it's something you highly value), then you'll probably go to places (looking your best) where you might meet someone special. If you perceive yourself as lacking wealth, then you'll examine methods that help you earn or save more money. If you're lacking friends, then you'll join a group or find other ways to meet people.

Ryk Neethling is an Olympic gold medalist in swimming. By all reports, he spends most of his waking hours in the pool improving his technique. He's preoccupied and thinks about his performance whenever he's not swimming, and he has tremendous discipline in this area. Ryk has won numerous awards in his sport, he loves to talk about swimming, and his dreams and visualizations revolve around moving swiftly and powerfully through the water. The goals that are foremost in his mind are directly related to his career as a swimmer.

It's no mystery: swimming excellence is Ryk's highest value.

Where did this value come from? When he was six years old, Ryk nearly drowned. This experience may have inspired him to become a great swimmer so he could excel in the water and ensure that the past didn't repeat itself. So the "void" from his childhood (his lack of proficient swimming skills) appears to have become his highest value.

Whenever you feel like your life is missing something, you may notice a strong desire to fill the void. *Fulfillment* means "the process of filling, or making full." You fulfill your voids by either transforming how you see the world or through the actions you take. You'll go after whatever is highest on your values list and focus on achieving it. If something is a lower value, then you probably won't take the time to seek it because it's not quite as important to you.

These voids—what's missing or unfulfilled—can be found in any of the seven areas of life. (I'll refer to these throughout, so it's a good idea to bookmark this page so that you can refer back to this list as needed.) The seven areas are as follows:

1. **Spiritual** (connection or cause)
2. **Mental** (intellect or knowledge)
3. **Vocational** (career success)
4. **Financial** (wealth)
5. **Familial** (relationships)

6. **Social** (connections and friendships)
7. **Physical** (well-being and vitality)

Actually, everything you might seek is already present in your life, but it's in a form you don't yet recognize. Zen masters teach that as soon as you stop searching outside of yourself, you can find what you desire, as it has always existed within your sphere of awareness and influence. As soon as you acknowledge, honor, and appreciate the form in which your value has already been fulfilled (where it already exists in your life), you have the power to transform it. On the other hand, when you perceive and act as if you're constantly lacking, what you desire will continue to evade you.

For instance, those who are overweight will be hard-pressed to find true well-being without first embracing the energy resources already present in a body that's been fed to fullness. People who long for romance will remain lonely if they can't find the love in being alone—that is, the fulfillment and contentment they have already surrounded themselves with as individuals. Those who crave material wealth won't get as far as they might want to until they recognize the areas in which they are already quite prosperous. And so on.

Sounds tricky, doesn't it? It isn't, really—it just takes the willingness to look at things from a new perspective. The rest of this chapter will guide you in exploring the different ways your hierarchy of values influences your experiences, shapes your perception of life, and ultimately determines your path to living your inspired destiny.

What Is the Order of Your Values?

Just about everyone has the desire to grow in all seven areas of life and reach his or her full potential. I've never met anyone who wakes up in the morning and wants to "shrink" by becoming less successful, knowledgeable, beautiful, or enthusiastic. Because of this desire to evolve, there's usually more than one thing that people perceive to be missing or unfulfilled.

Whenever there's more than one area you'd love to work on (that is, more than one area where you're seeking growth and fulfillment), you'll have more than one value, and some will be more important to you than others. In fact, by paying attention to what you're actually doing with your time, attention, energy, and environment, you can rank these values from most to least important (something you'll be asked to do later in this book). When you realize that there's a hierarchy to your priorities or values, you will better understand the impact they have on the ways in which you think and act.

Your values hierarchy determines how you perceive the world through your physical senses (your sight, hearing, taste, smell, and touch) and how you respond through your physical motor functions (what you do). You make every single decision according to this hierarchy. You decide to be part of the activities and opportunities that you think will give you the *greatest* degree of fulfillment in your highest values and, therefore, your life. And you also decide to turn down the activities and opportunities that you think will give you the *least* fulfillment in your highest values (and, therefore, your life).

When you live according to your lower values—working to satisfy someone else's idea of what should be most important to you, for example—you become uninspired and require continual outside motivation to stay focused on completing tasks. You feel disempowered, and life seems less meaningful. You sense that you're off track or lacking purpose, and you feel that you don't know what you ultimately want to dedicate your time and energy to. On the other hand, when you consciously live accordingly to your highest values, you become inspired, awakening your inner talents and hidden genius. You often feel expanded and fulfilled; and in such moments, your hierarchy of values dissolves. You perceive that nothing is, was, or ever will be "missing."

Attention Deficit Disorder vs. Attention Surplus Order

Imagine two friends, Joey and Melissa. Joey highly values baseball, exercise, computers, and healthy eating. Joey is single, and he's looking for young women he can take out to dinner and date. As you might expect, he invests a lot of time into his physical health and fitness, as well as being on the computer at home and work. Melissa, on the other hand, is studying journalism in college. She highly values her relationships and spends most of her spare time hanging out with her family and friends or studying.

Joey calls Melissa and asks her if she'd like to go to the mall with him that afternoon, as there's a sale at the local sports store he wants to check out. Melissa says she'd love to because she needs to pick up a gift for her cousin, who's celebrating his birthday that weekend.

While they're at the mall, Joey disappears into the sports store. Melissa becomes bored, distracted, and subdued as she experiences a form of "attention deficit disorder." She decides to leave and wait on a bench outside because what Joey's interested in doesn't intrigue her—in other words, his values aren't fulfilling for Melissa according to what her highest values are. Meanwhile, Joey is in the store looking at baseball gear and sports memorabilia. He feels alive, awake, and enthusiastic because he's taking action toward fulfilling his highest values; he's experiencing a form of "attention surplus order."

While Melissa is sitting on the bench, she notices a store where she can find study guides that will help her with her upcoming exams. She pops her head into the sports store and tells Joey that she's going to duck into the bookstore quickly and see if they have a title she's been looking for. Now Melissa is the one who comes alive. Soon enough, when Joey has to wait for her, he starts showing signs of attention deficit disorder because his highest value isn't studying or journalism. Yet Melissa now has a relative attention surplus order because education is high up in her values hierarchy.

You also experience both aspects of attention deficit disorder and surplus order. Nobody has to get you up in the morning to act according to your highest values. Your lowest values, though? You'll be hitting the snooze button repeatedly! When you're learning about a topic that's interesting to you (also known as a high value), you are diligent and focused. When you can clearly see how doing well in something will assist you in getting where you want to be in life, you master it no matter what it takes. You seek out all the information that will enable you to achieve your higher valued outcome.

On the other hand, when you're learning about a topic or discipline that you can't really relate to and don't see how it helps you fulfill your highest values, then you're very likely to experience challenges. You'll be less focused, get easily frustrated, and have a tendency to procrastinate.

Your top priorities (your highest values) inspire you from within. You're most disciplined, reliable, and organized whenever you're addressing those priorities. (You're most distracted, chaotic, and undisciplined when it comes to your lower values.) Your highest values illuminate a vision for your life, and you feel content and on track when you're working toward them.

How Your Values Impact Memory

Your hierarchy of values not only determines where you have the greatest or least amount of focus in the different areas of life; but also determines your ability to remember information, people, places, and events.

Let's say you meet someone whom you're pretty certain you'll never want to see again. This person has no obvious value to you, and you can't see how he or she will be of any service to you or assist you in achieving what's most important to you. By the time someone like that finishes telling you his or her name, you've already forgotten it. However, the second you meet someone you think will be important in your life, you mentally recite the name over and over again, and you seldom, if ever, forget it. You ask your new friend to repeat it to make sure that you've gotten it, and it goes into your long-term memory.

The same principle applies to opportunities, information, and other events in your experience. What you perceive that will fulfill your highest values goes into your long-term memory, but the things that don't fulfill your highest values are quickly discarded and forgotten.

When you have to acquire a new skill, for instance, and it isn't high on your values list, you may have a hard time learning it and will soon forget most of what you've been taught. Your instructor will probably become increasingly frustrated about having to constantly remind you how to perform the skill, and you may even be labeled "slow" or "lazy." The truth? The skill wasn't linked to your highest values, and you couldn't see how mastering it was going to help fulfill what's most important in your life. There's nothing wrong with that (or with you)—you just have a specific hierarchy of values that determines what will and won't become a part of your long-term memory.

Your Values Speed Up and Slow Down Time

It's said that Albert Einstein once mused that when you're sitting with a pretty girl, an hour feels like a minute, but when you're sitting on a hot stove, a minute feels like an hour. So true! Whenever you're doing something that feels fulfilling and you believe that it's supporting your highest values, time seems to fly by. But when you're doing something that feels uninspiring and you believe that it's of a lower value, the minutes drag.

You can usually talk to someone all night if the topic is important to you, but if someone's going on about something you don't care about, the conversation seems endless and you're stuck listening (or pretending to listen). Similarly, if you're on a date and you're having a great time chatting in the car with someone, it's as if you've been teleported to the restaurant or movie theater—the time just flies by and you don't even notice the drive. But if you're behind the wheel with someone you've just argued with, it feels like the longest ride you've ever taken, even if your destination is just a few blocks away. Indeed, some minutes feel like hours. It's all about your perception and values.

How You Identify with Your Values

If you're inspired by something and have devoted yourself to becoming the greatest you can be in that endeavor, then you'll identify with it: "I'm a student," "I'm a runner," "I'm a mom," "I'm a writer," "I'm a lawyer," "I'm a soldier," and so on. You'll filter the world through your values, spotting opportunities that assist you in achieving your goals.

For example, if you're inspired by hairdressing and have a part- or full-time job as a stylist, then you might find your attention drawn to the salons in your area that have more experienced and higher-paid staff. If someone asked what you do for a living, you'd say, "I'm a hairstylist." You notice completely different things in the world than someone who values anything other than what's highest among your priorities.

You also tend to "own" whatever is highest on your values and "disown" whatever is lowest. You want to be known, recognized, and remembered for doing what's important to you because you're naturally reliable, disciplined, and focused in those areas. As you go down your hierarchy list, though, you'll find that you have an increasing probability of experiencing procrastination, frustration, and indecision. You sit there with disorder and chaos, become frustrated with your life, and disown the tasks that are lower values. As I've mentioned earlier, when you aren't inspired by what you're doing, you require motivation to keep you focused on completing those tasks. The difference between motivation and inspiration is that motivation is required from the outside and is of the lowest values, and inspiration comes from within and is of the highest values. Living congruently with your highest values is the key to experiencing greater degrees of fulfillment across all seven areas of life.

You increase the likelihood of doing what you love and revealing your inspired destiny when you focus on your highest values. The more clearly you see what's important to you, the easier you're able to set goals. Living a purposeful life means having certainty and living in alignment with your highest priorities.

In the next chapter, you'll get to know your values and their unique hierarchy—an essential key to discovering your life's purpose and determining your direction for the future.

Inspired Insights

- Your values are based on what you perceive as "missing" in your life.

- Your values can be ranked in order of importance; this is known as your "hierarchy of values."

- You make every decision according to your hierarchy of values.

- Your highest values determine where you have the greatest amount of attention, long-term memory, focus, discipline, dedication, and inspiration.

- Living congruently with your authentic hierarchy of values increases the likelihood of discovering your purpose and living a fulfilling and meaningful life.

Words of Power

Choose at least one of the following affirmations and repeat it to yourself every day for at least the next month (ideally for the next few months). If this seems particularly challenging (or particularly rewarding), make a commitment to repeat it to yourself every day for the rest of your life.

I know and honor my authentic values in life.

I make decisions according to my highest values.

My unconscious voids drive my conscious hierarchy of values.

I am inspired from within as I live congruently with my highest values.

CHAPTER 3

What Is Most Important to You?

*"When your values are clear to you,
making decisions becomes easier."*
— **Roy Disney**

Knowing your hierarchy of values is absolutely essential for discovering your purpose and revealing your destiny. When you know what is most important to you and you honor it, you gain certainty about what you want to dedicate your life to being, doing, and having.

The following several pages contain The Demartini Value Determination Process™, which will assist you in identifying and defining your values. To complete the process, take out a notebook or journal and write down your top-three answers to the questions in each section. Once you've finished, follow the instructions at the end of the chapter.

1. How Do You Fill Your Space?

Look around your home, your office, and any other physical environments where you spend time. You've naturally filled these places with things that represent what you highly value. Identify the objects that mean the most to you, and think about how they demonstrate your values. For example, your living room might have books, magazines, or newspapers on topics that interest you; trophies and awards from sports or academics; posters of the figures or artwork that inspire you; and/or framed photos of your family, friends, or partner. Examine your surroundings and ask yourself how the objects you see reveal what you hold dear. What do you learn about yourself based on these possessions?

If you could see the places where I spend my time, for instance, you'd notice books, a computer, various research materials, luggage, and clothes. To me, these items demonstrate that traveling, researching, writing, and teaching are most important in my life. Keenly observe the places where you spend the most time, and find out how your surroundings clue you in on your highest values. Things that are unimportant end up in the trash, attic, or garage. But what you truly care for will be on display for you (and the world) to see.

2. How Do You Spend Your Time?

You make time for your highest values but put off whatever is lowest. Observe how you currently carve up your day, and note what you do and how long you do it. What do you spend the most amount of time on? What do you spend your time doing every chance you get?

Let's look at a student who claims that her highest value is education. But when she honestly tracked how she spends her time, her day looked like this:

- Wake up late and rush to get ready for school
- Socialize with peers during classes (6 hours)
- Play sports with friends after school (3 hours)
- Eat dinner with family (1 hour)
- Watch TV and play video games before bed (3 hours)

According to the above list, it doesn't seem like formal education is this student's highest value. In truth, we see that socializing comes first, and sports and relaxing come second. Formal studying or classroom learning isn't even mentioned—in addition, she struggles to wake up on time to start her day. So formal education actually ranks among the lowest values in her hierarchy.

A lot of people tell me (or themselves) that their highest value is something other than what it really is because of what they think it "should" be. Realize that just because something that's seemingly important isn't what you highly value, it doesn't mean that you completely discredit it; it just may not be your top value. Sometimes you put other people on pedestals and inject their values into your life and try to live according to who they are, instead of honoring your authentic self. Even if you don't recognize this, you will *still* live according to your *own* higher values, but you'll feel unfulfilled and uninspired because you'll have unrealistic expectations.

Ask yourself how you *actually* allocate the hours in a day. What is so important that you make time for it daily because it fulfills you? What comes in second and third?

3. How Do You Spend Your Energy?

When you do what you love, you feel energized and pumped. However, you feel tired whenever you're doing something associated with a lower value because you can't see how it helps you fulfill what is most important to you.

Let's say you're 17 years old and you highly value your social life. It's Saturday afternoon, yet you're sitting around feeling bored and kind of drained. Then one of your friends calls and says, "Let's go to a party tonight!" You immediately have more than enough energy. On the other hand, if your parents say, "Let's go clean up the garage," you may try to get out of it or put it off because you're tired. Is that because you're lazy? No. You just don't value a clean garage as much as you value having fun with friends. (Or, for that matter, as much as your parents do.)

Which activities and tasks do you have plenty of energy for? What makes you come alive? Ask yourself: *Where do I love to spend most of my energy during the day, week, or month? What do I love to focus on and pour myself into?*

When you're doing what you love and loving what you do, you require less sleep and express more vitality and vigor. You consistently have energy for your highest values.

4. How Do You Spend Your Money?

In his book *Principles of Economics,* Alfred Marshall emphasized that people spend their money according to their values—and the principles still hold true, more than 100 years after its publication in 1890. If you place value on saving because you really want to be wealthy in 5, 10, or 15 years, then you'll put away funds before you pay your bills or other expenses. If you don't value saving, you'll spend money on whatever you perceive to be more important, and you'll usually run out of cash before the end of the week or month.

How you spend has nothing to do with how much money you make; it has everything to do with your priorities. Many people who have earned meager salaries still found ways to save and eventually amassed quite a bit of wealth. Likewise, many who have raked in millions but put away little of it (purchasing houses, cars, yachts, clothes, and so on) did so because what they bought was connected to their highest values.

What do you do with your money? Do you spend it on clothes, education, or travel? Do you throw parties or buy rounds of drinks when you're out? Do you save money so you can eventually attain specific things, such as a car or a house? Do you spend money on a gym membership, or perhaps on gifts for your family? You invest in whatever is most important to you, and whenever you receive money, you'll spend it according to your values hierarchy.

5. Where Are You Most Organized?

Your areas of highest value will be the most ordered parts of your life, containing little or no chaos. However, you require motivation to get you to take care of your lower values, the areas in which you're less organized. (Interestingly, the people who are closest to you will tend to place a higher value on those things that are of lower importance to you. Therefore, they tend to have control over you in the areas where you're disorganized.)

For example, you might have order in your social life: You know who knows who, who their families are and where they live, and what everyone does for a living. When you're at a party or other social gathering, you know who to introduce to whom and who will get along with each other. The contacts in your phone book are well organized and up-to-date, complete with people's nicknames and birthdays. You exhibit order in this area of your life, indicating that relationships rank high in your values.

What aspects of your life are most organized? That is, where do things run smoothly, with the greatest amount of detail? These areas demonstrate that they are highly valued. Wherever you experience chaos and disorganization, however, this reveals the areas that are low on your values hierarchy.

6. Where Are You Most Disciplined?

As I've mentioned, you can easily focus on what you truly care about. Whenever you label yourself as someone who is *undisciplined, unsettled,* or *flighty,* know that this indicates that what you're doing isn't something that ranks high in your values. It's an unrealistic expectation that you'll live outside of your hierarchy of values. When you work toward achieving your genuine goals, you'll be naturally disciplined and enthusiastic.

Where are you most disciplined? That is, where do you show up and take action every time without fail? What can other people always count on you to do? Where are you consistently on task and totally accountable?

7. *What Do You Think About?*

When something is a high value for you, it fills up time and space in your mind; in other words, you frequently think about what is most important. When people discuss something that is a low value for you (but high for them, obviously, since they're talking about it), your mind may begin to wander and return to topics that are of more interest to you. Know that your thoughts naturally drift to your highest values.

You might spend all your time thinking about traveling to exotic places, going shopping at the end of the week, or playing your best golf game on the weekend with your friends. Maybe you think about what you'd really love to do with your life, or perhaps your thoughts are primarily on seeing your partner or planning activities with your family during the holidays. Whatever is consistently in your mind indicates what is high among your values.

What do you think about most? When your mind wanders, where does it go? When you're contemplative, what do you see in your mind's eye? The consistent, long-term thoughts and musings indicate your highest values.

8. What Do You Visualize?

In your mind, you envision something for yourself. You have a dream about how you'd love your life to unfold, and you focus on it regularly. If you are a musician, for example, you probably spend time imagining yourself rehearsing or playing onstage at your next gig. You might hear your music and gaze upon the audience loving the show. Maybe you can see the number of tickets sold to those wanting to come to your concert.

If you place a high value on building financial wealth, you might visualize the figures in your bank or investment account and how much your savings increase every week, month, and year. You might see what the grand total will be in the future, and envision the things you would do with your wealth. These images and real-life plans reveal what you care most about.

What do you imagine for yourself? What's your vision? When you daydream about the future, what's the recurring theme? Your visualizations express your highest values and what you're most focused on bringing into reality.

9. What Do You Talk to Yourself About?

You—like everyone else—engage in self-talk, words that have the ability to build you up and tear you down. Through both of these sides, you engage in an ongoing, internal dialogue regarding your highest values.

You might be talking to yourself about what decision to make, which opportunities would yield the greatest rewards, or what skills would be the most valuable to assist you in fulfilling your goals. You might be planning for the upcoming week, month, or year. Perhaps you're talking to yourself about a past performance and ways in which you can refine your actions in the future. Maybe you're coaching yourself about which moves to make in your next game or tournament. You might even be making plans for the weekend with your friends or family.

What do you talk to yourself about most? What is the subject or topic that pops up frequently during your internal dialogue? Remember that what you talk about reflects what's truly important to you and what you'd love to create more of or find a way to achieve. The affirmations and statements you recite reveal whatever is highest on your values hierarchy.

10. What Do You Talk to Other People About?

When it comes to your highest values, you become extroverted. In other words, you love talking to people about what inspires you. You may even notice a tendency to bring conversations around to the topics that matter most to you.

Next time you're in a social setting, pay attention to how everyone (with their own unique hierarchy of values) will direct the conversation toward the subjects that are most important to them. Those who highly value their social lives might ask what you did the past weekend, for example. But if socializing is lower on your values hierarchy and earning money is higher, then you might say, "I didn't go to any parties, but I went to work on Sunday and earned $500. What type of financial plans are you investing in for the future?"

When you find someone who has similar values, you'll often find that you can stay up late talking about your common interests. On the other hand, when you're conversing with someone whose values clash with yours (in relation to your hierarchy), you might find that you both try to change the subject or even avoid chatting with each other.

When you meet someone new, what do you find yourself discussing? What conversations captivate you for the longest periods? What could you easily stay up all night talking about?

11. What Inspires You?

Throughout your life, you've had experiences that profoundly inspired you. They may have even been so moving that they brought tears to your eyes. Whether they've been initiated by others or yourself, and regardless of when they took place, these events opened your mind and heart to the possibilities of fulfilling what is truly most important in your life.

Often your heroes have been those who have demonstrated the values that hold the most meaning for you. Recall the moments or situations when you were deeply inspired, and look for commonalities among them. What is the theme? What truly inspires you? When you uncover this, you can determine what is highest on your list of values.

12. What Are Your Goals?

Take a moment right now and make a list of your current goals. What are you working toward? Think of the seven areas of life and where your objectives fit: Are your goals based on saving money so you can buy something you would really love to have? Are they focused on the future you want to have with your partner? Traveling and taking an extended vacation with family or friends? Changing your job or career?

Know that there's a correlation between the goals you set and what is most important to you. When your social life ranks high among your values, for example, you set goals relating to your friends, gatherings and parties, and perhaps people you'd love to meet. If you value learning and expanding your mind, you set goals in academics or find ways to create more educational opportunities for yourself. If you're focused on your job or plan to start a business someday, you set goals related to your career advancement. If your financial aspirations rank high, you set goals that will help you maximize your savings and earnings. And if your highest values revolve around your body, you set goals related to your health and well-being.

Consider what you would most love to be, do, or have in your life. Which of your goals are most meaningful and important? What are your top-three goals for the future? What are the most consistent, long-term aspirations you've worked toward? Are they manifesting in your reality right now?

How Do You Write Your Hierarchy of Values?

Once you've read through the 12 values determinants and have answered all of the questions, you can now begin putting together your initial hierarchy of values. Go to the first value you wrote down, and count how many times it (or its equivalent) turned up in the rest of your responses. For instance, you may have written *studying* for the question about how you spend your time, *learning* for how you spend your energy, and *books* for what fills your living space. These point to "expanding your mental capacities" or "understanding and learning" as a value. So tally them up, and jot down the number next to that value, however you decide to word it. Repeat the process for the second value you wrote, then the third one, and so on.

Now that you've counted and classified them, you can put them in numerical order. The top five to nine values (in the sequence they showed up in) give you a pretty clear picture of your values hierarchy.

You're wise to double-check yourself. Make sure that your voids and values are congruent. Your highest value will be the same as what you perceive as most "missing" in life—what you'd dearly love to have "more" of. The second highest will be what you perceive as the second-most "missing," and so on. If you don't think your values and voids match up like this, revisit the 12 determinants and your responses to the questions.

An example of your hierarchy of values might look like this:

1. **Socializing:** spending time with my friends

2. **Studying and learning:** educating myself in my field of choice

3. **Relationship:** seeing and talking to my partner

4. **Family:** spending time with my family on weekends

5. **Working:** focusing on my job and career

6. **Physical fitness:** exercising regularly and keeping fit

7. **Spirituality:** praying and counting my blessings daily

Your top values may not be what you assumed or wanted them to be; however, your list reveals what is significant in your life right now. If you had one recurring theme that showed up on most of the values determinants, it means that in this moment, this particular item is clearly important. This is where you spend most of your time, money, energy, and so on.

What you assume or think you want and what you actually live by could be two very different things, and this becomes apparent once you determine your hierarchy. What you *think* you want may actually be influenced by the values of those you've given authority to. Most people are unaware of what their real values are, and instead, they've developed unrealistic expectations that don't match what their genuine life goals are.

Whenever you adopt an unrealistic fantasy, you might try to change yourself into someone or something you aren't. Then when you naturally continue to live according to what is *truly* important to you, you beat yourself up for not being who you believe you should or acting how you think you should.

In every moment, your decisions and actions demonstrate your higher values. You consistently live according to your hierarchy. You'll "sacrifice" whatever relates to your lower values for whatever relates to your higher ones. (In the next part of this book, however, you'll learn how to change your authentic hierarchy so that you can empower other—or all—aspects of your life.)

Since what you're perceiving as missing drives your values, see if you can identify what in your past may have created a void for the things you value today. (Remember that your voids are what you perceive as most "missing" in life.)

When I was a toddler, for example, I had a brace to correct bone deformities in my leg and foot. By the time I was four, though, I wanted out of that restrictive thing! I begged my father to remove it and promised to work very hard to keep my foot straight. I felt constrained by the brace, and it was difficult to watch other kids run and play while I hobbled around on my bum leg. So when my parents and doctor finally "liberated" me, I ran every chance I got! I'd run down the street, and I'd run to school and back . . . just because I could. I practiced keeping my foot straight and worked on increasing my speed, and because of my constant attention to this value (running), I became one of the fastest kids in my school.

By the time my first-grade teacher pronounced me hopelessly learning disabled, I'd already turned to sports. It was one place where I felt totally unrestrained, as if I could go anywhere and do anything at my own pace.

Nowadays, I think that my way of fulfilling this value of being "fast and free" has transformed into my love of traveling. More than 360 days of the year, I'm going somewhere—meeting new people and teaching them how to empower their lives. Not being tied to a particular place still gives me that sensation of freedom, and my journeys are something I highly value.

What do you perceive as most missing in your life? (That is what you most value.) What is the correlation between what appears to be missing and your current values? Remember that without the perception of emptiness, there could be no concept of fulfillment.

Your Ever-Changing Hierarchy of Values

As you grow and mature, your hierarchy of values will change. Your values shift over time as you achieve goals and overcome challenges in life. Once you feel that something is no longer "missing," you'll move on to whatever your next biggest void may be. You'll never run out of voids or values to focus on, as a new void will surface every time you fulfill a value.

Since your values change and realign themselves over time, it's wise to reevaluate what is important to you on a regular basis to stay on top of your priorities. Set some time aside every three months to complete this process. Become clear on your values now and you'll begin to actively design your future, setting your goals according to what is truly important to you.

Discovering your values hierarchy is the key because it will be so much easier for you to follow your destined path. Harmony with your authentic values unlocks the doorway to your purpose and your inspired destiny.

Inspired Insights

- You can discover your highest values by examining what you fill your space with; how you spend your time, energy, and money; where you're most organized and disciplined; what you think about and visualize; what you talk to yourself and others about; what inspires you; and what your top goals are.

- Your highest value will be the same as what you perceive as most "missing" in your life.

- Your hierarchy of values reflects what is truly important to you right now.

- What you think your values are and what they actually are can be two very different things.

- Your hierarchy of values will change throughout life as you fulfill what is most important to you. You'll never run out of voids and values.

Words of Power

Choose at least one of the following affirmations and repeat it to yourself every day for at least the next month (ideally for the next few months). If this seems particularly challenging (or particularly rewarding), make a commitment to repeat it to yourself every day for the rest of your life.

I know what my highest values in life are
and I appreciate and honor them.

I set goals according to my highest and most authentic values.

I fulfill my life by living in alignment with my highest values.

I live a meaningful and inspiring life.

CHAPTER 4

Your Values Drive Your Purpose

"You are what your deep, driving desire is.
As your desire is, so is your will. As your will is,
so is your deed. As your deed is, so is your destiny."
— **The Upanishads**

You may expect to wake up one morning with a divine revelation that suddenly makes you crystal clear on what you want to do every day for the rest of your life. Some people—about one to three percent—do experience a defining moment like this, usually at an early age, and many others realize their purpose during adulthood. Still, some spend their entire lives searching for a more meaningful existence yet can never quite awaken to or acknowledge it.

Perceiving yourself as directionless can be frustrating and stressful, but those strong emotions can be useful and ultimately help you achieve what you're truly after. You judge, ridicule, or beat yourself up when you feel unsure about who you are, and this is the result of two unwise choices: 1) holding on to unrealistic expectations, and 2) aligning yourself with someone else's values instead of your own.

If you're engaged in this kind of self-flagellation, it's time to break through that mind-set and identify *your* highest values. When you do so, you're able to see that *you're already living according to what's most important to you*—you just haven't realized it yet. So it may be time to honestly answer one of the most challenging and rewarding life questions: *What would I truly love to be and do?*

What Is the Truth about Your Purpose?

What is *your* unique purpose? How do you uncover it? When you honestly evaluate your life as it is today—*not* as you think it should be—according to the value-determination process you read in the previous chapter, you'll know with more certainty what resides at the top of your values hierarchy. Then it's just a matter of acknowledging that you're seeking what you perceive is most missing, and your purpose is to fulfill those voids with the greatest number of values.

Your life mission is to achieve this very outcome. **Your purpose is the summation of your hierarchy of values, specifically your top-five values.** Your number one value is most important—what ancient Greeks called *telos,* or "ultimate end." The rest are the means to this end. When you continually evaluate and examine your hierarchy, it's known as *axiology,* the study of value and worth. When you live in harmony with your values, you experience the greatest self-worth.

As I've mentioned, what you might assume or think your life purpose is may be an unrealistic idealism you've absorbed (consciously or unconsciously) from those you admire—it's what others believe is important. You can try to live accordingly to their views, but your actions will always be a constant reflection of whatever is highest among your values as they stand at that moment. Remember that your actions and inactions reveal your purpose every time. *So study them!*

Now here's something that may come as a surprise or challenge your current perceptions, so read it carefully: **Because you**

are making every decision and acting upon all opportunities and relationships to fulfill your highest values, it is impossible for you to be off purpose. In other words, you're consistently doing things that are highest on your values hierarchy, so you *are* inwardly aware of your destiny—there's no such thing as someone who doesn't know his or her purpose. You may be choosing not to reveal it to yourself because you're afraid of being held account-able and possibly failing to achieve your dream, but deep within, you do know what your unique purpose is.

It's also not possible for you to uncover your purpose and then feel uninspired by it, for you have unlimited inspiration in the areas of your highest values. You are naturally inspired about liv-ing your purpose, and this is what gives your life meaning. Other people may look at your life and think you have an abundance of whatever you are seeking, but you still perceive it as missing and are driven to fulfill it.

Your Purpose and the Seven Areas of Life

As mentioned earlier, there are seven areas of life that hold the keys to uncovering your destiny. Here they are again:

1. **Spiritual:** awareness, wisdom, religious and/or spiritual causes, connection to God/Universe

2. **Mental:** genius, knowledge, information and expertise, an expanded mind

3. **Vocational:** professional fulfillment, job and career success

4. **Financial:** accumulation of wealth and/or initiation of philanthropic causes

5. **Familial:** fulfilling relationships with family, rituals and traditions, intimacy with a partner

6. **Social:** influence, leadership, networks, friendships

7. **Physical:** vitality, energy, stamina, well-being, confidence, attractiveness

Your purpose can be related to one or more of the seven areas of life and can reveal your inspired destiny. Confusion about what you would love to do with your life isn't about a lack of options (thousands of possibilities exist in the seven areas); rather, it's about finding what's most aligned with your highest values.

Researching the biographies of people who have made an impact on the world through living and fulfilling their purpose can assist you in clarifying your own direction. Here are several examples to help get you started.

Spiritual Purpose

Mother Teresa and the Dalai Lama dedicated their lives to spiritual service. These unique individuals have touched the world through their actions, spreading a message from their hearts and providing hope and inspiration to millions of people. In Western culture, Wayne Dyer and Deepak Chopra are regarded as great spiritual teachers who live inspiring, fulfilling lives.

If your highest values are in this area, then your purpose may be to serve as a spiritual healer or teacher, write inspirational stories or studies, or touch the world through your religious beliefs or philosophy of living. Your purpose may have you seeking an ever-greater integration or connection with yourself, as well as the world around you. Your destiny might be to create a ministry or monastery, or build great temples and spiritual centers to provide people with a place to rejuvenate, meditate, and become present.

Mental Purpose

Many great achievers throughout history—such as Albert Einstein and Sir Isaac Newton—pursued their purpose through the power of the mind. My own purpose has a great focus here, as I travel the world and teach people how the mind works and ways to empower all seven areas of their lives. The philosopher Immanuel Kant knew his purpose at age 22, declaring: "I have already fixed upon the line which I am resolved to keep. I will enter on my course, and nothing shall prevent me from pursuing it."

Purpose in the mental aspect of life may mean studying and researching topics that inspire you with the goal of becoming a sought-after authority in your chosen field. Your mental purpose might also mean training and refining yourself as a leading educator on any level, from your family to your community, your country, or the world. Your greatest inspiration may be the challenge of breaking through paradigms to bring about a new perspective and world vision. Or it could involve solving global problems and answering humanity's most important questions.

Vocational Purpose

An inspired individual, Richard Branson has realized many great achievements through his vocational purpose. Famous for founding Virgin Atlantic Airways and Virgin Records, he is a leading-edge entrepreneur who focuses relentlessly on innovation and creating popular brands for his businesses. Branson's latest project is Virgin Galactic, the world's first "spaceline" that will take passengers to destinations off planet Earth and enable affordable suborbital space tourism.

Purpose in the vocational area of life might involve building a business and serving people through an inspired product, service, or idea. You might have a dream to become a successful entrepreneur who brings new products to the market in innovative ways.

Or perhaps you wish to devote yourself to mastering your trade or sharing your talents through products, services, or ideas (as the famous consultant and author Peter Drucker had done).

Your vocational purpose could also involve greatly refining your chosen career path. You may be inspired to make changes in your immediate environment (such as your community, city, state, or nation); or discover your desire to serve more of humanity by spreading your message or knowledge throughout the world to make a difference in the lives of millions.

Financial Purpose

A financial purpose can take on many shapes and forms in an inspired destiny. Warren Buffett and Bill Gates, who have amassed billions of dollars in personal and professional wealth, are good examples. Your purpose might involve raising money for projects or business concepts that inspire you or becoming a famous philanthropist like George Soros or any of the increasing number of millionaires and billionaires who have become much more involved in charitable causes.

You could feel compelled to master the art of building wealth, so you dedicate your life to studying accounting and economics. Perhaps your cause is to assist and empower others so that they can achieve financial independence in the long term.

Familial Purpose

Rose Kennedy had an inspiring mission statement regarding the familial area of her life: "My mission is to raise a family of world leaders." Equally inspiring, the First Lady of Qatar has dedicated herself to raising the standards of education for young people throughout the world.

A familial purpose might involve being dedicated to raising a family with your partner and devoting yourself to providing your children with the greatest life possible. You might be inspired to focus on creating a fulfilling relationship with your partner. Your purpose might also include conducting workshops or seminars on how to build powerful, loving relationships with family members or intimate partners.

Social Purpose

A great example of someone who has a purpose in the social area of life is Oprah Winfrey, who is most known for creating one of the highest-rated, most-watched television talk shows in American history. Your social purpose might be to establish a powerful networking platform for people all over the world. You may also be drawn to organizing functions, sales, company events, or other avenues for connecting people personally and/or professionally.

This life purpose might take you into the world of social entrepreneurship—for example, raising money and donating funds to help people in developing countries elevate their standard of living. You might dream of uniting large numbers of people to form social movements that stand for what you believe in so that you can achieve something amazing together. Your purpose could involve becoming the leader of a new trend that spreads quickly around the world. Being a charismatic speaker and influencing others with a powerful message from your heart is also an example of having a purpose in the social area of life.

Physical Purpose

Whether your goal is to become the next Lance Armstrong or Miss Universe, a physical purpose could take you anywhere in health and wellness from training to performing, dancing, modeling, and more. Because of my love for teaching and healing, I spent nine years practicing as a doctor of chiropractic, specializing in spinal conditions and the mind-body relationship. I built one of the larger chiropractic centers in the U.S., and my purpose had me putting my hands on hundreds of people each week, realigning their spines and physical systems, as well as inspiring their minds.

Building muscle strength and stamina and entering competitions for sports or bodybuilding might also be your physical purpose in life. Or perhaps you have dreams of organizing races or walks in your community or starting a healthy-cooking club with your neighbors.

Clarifying Your Inspired Purpose

Whichever of the seven areas of life your purpose is most strongly connected to, *you know what you would love to do with your life.* An awareness exists deep within you that helps you recognize the patterns and themes that reveal your ultimate purpose. Ask yourself what your mind seeks to fulfill: *What is the void that my mind perceives, and what do I desire to experience again and again? What am I most inspired by? What would I love to wake up and do every single day?* Remember that everyone has a meaningful purpose in life.

Sometimes you might allow your fears to creep in and keep you from consciously feeling that you're living according to your priorities, and this can cause stress and a sense of purposelessness. Later in this book, we'll explore the seven primary fears that prevent you from revealing your purpose and how to break through each one so that you can fulfill your inspired destiny. For now, know that even when your fears appear to be getting in the way, your authentic hierarchy of values is still running the show and guiding you toward what you would ultimately love to do or achieve.

Of course, life will bring you many touching or moving experiences. In those moments, you may also feel tears of inspiration welling up from your heart. That overwhelming gratitude is from your innermost mind letting you know that you're on track and in tune with your highest values. Allow those illuminated parts of yourself to guide you in revealing and refining your destiny. Pay attention to what you know you genuinely love to spend your time, energy, money, and thoughts doing. Keep a record of these glimmering moments, for they'll serve as milestones that help you become more certain of your future.

The sharper your purpose is—and the more aligned it is with what yearns to express itself from within your heart and mind—the more you will focus on fulfilling it. Your confidence increases when you're clear on your purpose. When you're tuned in to your inspired destiny, your direction becomes less puzzling, less variable, and more stable. When you know what you'd love to do, you more willingly embrace any obstacles on the path to creating an inspired life.

Exercise: Get Inspired!

Write Your Purpose Statement

Writing your purpose statement is a powerful way of integrating your discoveries about your highest values and what you would love to dedicate your life to. As I've mentioned, your inspired life is something that you already know and feel in your heart. It's a calling coming from inside of you, summoning you to do what you love (and it may be something that has grown out of an experience as far back as your childhood). Review your hierarchy of values, and look where it points you.

What you do know will expand as you get going, and the details of your purpose and the things that you don't fully know or understand will eventually become clear. Keep editing and refining your statement until you feel inspired and energized whenever you read it, share it with others, or even think about it.

Here are some steps to get you started:

1. Open a new document on your computer (or take out your journal or a few sheets of paper).

2. Examine your hierarchy of values.

3. Recall the moments in your life that have inspired you the most.

4. Consider that your life demonstrates whatever is truly most important to you. What do you notice?

5. Look for common themes or characteristics among your heroes (those who inspire you the most).

6. Name the most meaningful actions you've taken or skills you've developed along your career path.

7. Based on all of the notes you've taken, start writing your initial purpose statement.

Here are some examples:

— *I hereby declare before myself and the world that my primary purpose in life is to master the art of playing guitar so that I can travel around the world sharing my music with thousands of people and providing high-quality entertainment.*

— *I hereby declare before myself and the world that my primary purpose in life is to cultivate an inspiring relationship with my lifelong partner, working through our challenges in order to create a loving home in which to raise a family.*

— I hereby declare before myself and the world that my primary purpose in life is to become a great teacher in the topics of my choice and open a school for those who would love to dedicate their lives to these teachings.

— I hereby declare before myself and the world that my primary purpose in life is to venture to the outer limits of space; to own the first hotel in outer space; and to provide services for traveling beyond Earth in style, safety, and comfort.

I've been refining my own purpose statement for nearly 40 years, and today it reads as follows:

I hereby declare before myself and the world that my purpose in life is to dedicate myself to being a teacher and philosopher specializing in human behavior and maximizing human awareness and potential. It is my destiny to travel the world, setting foot upon every country on the face of the earth, sharing my teachings and research findings, and assisting people in living inspiring and magnificent lives.

As you begin to express your purpose in writing, you'll find that at first it can be a little shaky, but over time it becomes increasingly stable and certain as you gain clarity. Say to yourself: *I am worthy of uncovering my magnificence.* Your inner magnificence emerges spontaneously when you attune to your highest values and, therefore, your purpose. Read your statement daily and update or refine it frequently to keep yourself inspired.

I started working on my purpose statement at age 17, and my life has never been the same. It has helped me achieve an inspired and blessed existence. I'm certain that by clarifying what *you* are inspired about, you too can create a life that you would truly love.

Identity Crises Are Hidden Blessings

As your hierarchy of values changes and transforms, you may experience an "identity crisis" or "identity transformation." You'll begin to question your purpose, your future plans, or even who you are. Identity transformations are simply signs that your values are changing and that you've fulfilled something that appeared to be missing with something else of higher value to you. Consider these moments as opportunities to redefine or refine your purpose and what you now wish to dedicate your time and energy to.

The clearer you are about your purpose, the more certainty, presence, gratitude, and poise you will have. You will also have more power to influence other people to be a part of your purpose and help you achieve your dream, whatever that may be. Welcome identity transformations when they come, and take advantage of the opportunity to reexamine and refine your purpose. Honor your values and set goals that inspire you to do what you love. When you appreciate yourself the way you are, you'll unlock your unique talents and genius.

Inspired Insights

- Your life purpose is to fulfill the greatest amount of voids with the greatest amount of values.

- Your purpose may include any one or all of the seven areas of life.

- Writing and refining your purpose statement over time will bring you greater clarity on what you ultimately would love to dedicate your time and energy to.

- Every phase of your life prompts you to become clearer on your inspired destiny.

- Identity transformations are opportunities to reshape and refine your direction.

Words of Power

Choose at least one of the following affirmations and repeat it to yourself every day for at least the next month (ideally for the next few months). If this seems particularly challenging (or particularly rewarding), make a commitment to repeat it to yourself every day for the rest of your life.

I am worthy of uncovering my magnificence.

I know what I would love to do in life, and I pursue it.

I can see my purpose in crystal clear detail.

My life is inspired by a great cause.

CHAPTER 5

Mastering the Art of Communication

"When you help other people get what they want in life, you get what you want in life."
— **Zig Ziglar**

To achieve what you would love out of life, you need to be an effective communicator. When you master this, you'll inspire others who will also help you realize your long- or short-term goals.

Communication, of course, means more than expressing yourself with words or facial expressions—rather, it implies that others *listen* and *understand* . . . they get you and you get them. So the *art* is the ability to communicate what is most important to you in terms of what is most important to others.

Mastering the art of communication will assist you in working with teachers, teammates, managers, sponsors, coaches, co-workers, employees, and anyone else who can help you excel. Powerful communication will also enable you to share your dreams with your family and build greater relationships with your friends and social networks. When you really care for others, you'll make sure that you take time to discover what their values and desires in life are and then relate your values to those.

You Have Opposite and Complementary
Values to Someone in the World

In the 5th century B.C., the Greek philosopher Heracleitus believed that for each person in the world, there existed someone who had the exact opposite values. In other words, there is an individual who is your complementary opposite: this person values exactly what you don't value, and whatever you want to achieve isn't what he or she wants to achieve. This means that there's always someone who sees things from the opposite point of view.

You tend to attract people into your life to help you fill in the gaps—those who value what's lower on your hierarchy so that you can learn to appreciate all the things that you currently don't. In this way, you'll get to love everything you experience and comprehend a variety of perspectives.

This practice was reemphasized by Aristotle, another Greek philosopher, and later the French essayist Montaigne when their writings revealed that there were opposites balancing out customs and conventions in society and within families.

Take a look at your own relatives and those of your friends, and you'll see that people tend to be paired by opposites. You'll discover, for example, that there will usually be an overachiever with an underachiever, a nomad with a homebody, and an academic with a nonacademic. You might sometimes wonder why your parents or siblings are so different from you, yet the truth is that they simply have their own specific hierarchy of values. Remember that you have distinct directions and desires that are not like any other person's in the world—they're as individual as fingerprints or retinal patterns.

All people are needed in the great social equation, and no one is right or wrong based upon his or her values hierarchy. In fact, you must have a unique order for the world to work, for the summation of all human behaviors make up the balance of love, just like particles and antiparticles in physics make up the balance that scientists call light.

Whatever parents have lowest among their values will usually be what their children tend to focus upon—that is, almost all children will automatically hold up what their mothers and fathers or other family members repress. What's most important to you will likely upset either one or both of your parents. This can often lead to disagreements or arguments, and unless your parents can communicate inside of your values, you won't be interested in what they say, and vice versa.

On the other hand, if you communicate what you'd love to do in terms of your mom and dad's values, they'll open up to you and give you freedom. If you remind them, for example, that you're on the honor roll or you're getting special recognition in sports, and then ask if you can borrow $20 to see a movie on Friday night with your friends, they are likely to say, "Sure, honey! We're so proud of you." (That's assuming your parents value your success in school.) However, if you say that you're on drugs (or are selling drugs), you stole their credit card, the police are chasing after you, and the path has led back to them . . . and then you ask your parents if you can borrow $20, it's likely that they'll swiftly kick you out of the house. (That's assuming your parents aren't in the mob.)

Parents will automatically establish stricter rules when their children challenge their values and loosen up when their values are supported. You do the same thing with all the people in your life, from your friends to your siblings, classmates and peers, colleagues, and even your partners. You make decisions according to your values, and they make decisions according to theirs. Because you, like every person, have a unique hierarchy, this means that you don't see the world the way it really is; instead, you view the world as it's filtered through your values.

This is why you may notice that some family members and friends are able to perceive things that you don't or can't (at least not in that moment). Together, the values of all the people in your life make up a more complete picture of the world. If everyone had the same values, there would be no individuals—if any two people were exactly the same, one wouldn't be necessary.

The key to relating to those around you (and vice versa) is making sure you honor their values and learning how to communicate your own in terms of theirs. Most people fall into the trap of believing that their values are best, which makes people who have different priorities somehow wrong or insignificant.

So whenever another person does something that you perceive supports your values, you'll be tempted to label that individual as "good" or "nice," and open up to him or her more easily. But when someone does something that seems to challenge your values, you'll be tempted to label the person as "bad" or "mean," and close down and withdraw. Still, you would be wise to avoid thinking that your values are better or more mature than others'. It just leads to assumptions that they'll eventually come around and adopt a values system just like yours . . . but that's highly unlikely!

Remember that nobody is right or wrong based upon his or her values hierarchy. All human beings want to be loved for who they are and what is important to them, just as you want to be loved and appreciated for who you are. Resist the urge to try to change people—instead, stay focused on and celebrate who they truly are.

Understanding the Differences Between
Careless, Careful, and Caring

Whenever you're in the mind-set that your values are right and other people's are wrong, you'll feel self-righteous, puff yourself up, strut around like a rooster, and start to project your beliefs onto others. That's being *careless:* you *care less* about others' values than you do about your own. Whenever you do this, you're going to run into resistance because trying to get people to do things that just aren't important to them usually proves to be unfruitful.

Others will stand up for their authentic values unless they're infatuated with you and have put you on a pedestal. If people have elevated you in this way, they'll tend to sacrifice their values and try to do things to please you. If they give up what's important to them, however, they must repress their true objectives, which leads to frustration and dissatisfaction. They will eventually resent you for projecting your values onto them instead of appreciating them for who they really are.

If *you* look up to others and inject their values into your own life, you're diminishing yourself. Instead of being careless, you're now walking on eggshells and being overly *careful.* You now care more about their values than you do your own. You try to become someone you aren't, always doing things to please another person. Anytime you minimize yourself in this way, you build resentment because you're sacrificing what is truly important in your life.

Both of these dynamics lead to "alternating monologues" instead of effective communication or dialogues. In other words, when you're talking, the other person isn't listening; instead, he or she is thinking about what to say next. And while the other person is talking, you're thinking about your next line and not really listening. This one-sided type of "conversation" gets little accomplished.

What happens if you realize that other people's values hierarchies are just as significant as yours and, in fact, are equal? You can communicate your values in a way that satisfies the values of others, and vice versa. If you help people get where they want to go in life, you get where you want to go in life, too . . . but you have to widen your perspective to learn how to do that.

Caring is what keeps relationships alive. Remember that your highest values represent your identity. No one really wants to be put on a pedestal and constantly feel pressured to live up to someone else's expectations. People don't want to be someone they're not—and they can't really do it, anyway.

Chicks Dig Smart Guys

I once met with a 19-year-old man whose father had contacted me with a request to "fix" his son. As the dad explained, "He's not doing well in school, he's not focused or disciplined, and he's out every night getting stoned. I want him to be successful in economics and business, but he's screwing it all up." The father insinuated that his son might also have a learning problem, and he asked if I could help out.

"Absolutely," I assured him. When I met with his son, we talked about his values, where he went to school, and what he was interested in. Then I asked, "What's the most important thing in your life right now?"

He smiled. "Chicks! You know . . . girls."

"Okay. What else is really important to you?"

"Just chicks!" (Well, he *was* a 19-year-old with raging hormones. What else was he going to be interested in?)

I then made a list of all the courses he was taking at the time and wrote down his highest value ("chicks/girls"). Then I started to ask him a series of questions.

"What do you think women like?" He thought they were into shopping and successful guys. So I asked him what he was doing to maximize his wealth and intelligence—the barometers of the kind of success, according to him, that women like. (Not to mention the same barometers of success that his father used.)

The young man knew where I was coming from. "My father wants me to be financially successful."

"And he's getting annoyed because he thinks you aren't meeting his expectations anymore, according to what's important to him?"

"Yeah. And if I get cut off, I'm screwed!"

We talked about his study habits and course load for a while, and I told him about two types of women: admirers and rescuers. Admirers would be attracted to his intelligence, and rescuers would be delighted to spend time with him if he humbly asked them to help him study. I pointed out that if he approached a woman (perhaps the most attractive and intelligent one in his classes) and sincerely asked for her help, her values might just be turned on by those two mechanisms of intelligence and sincerity. So if he studied hard and did well in school, he would attract the attention of half the women he was interested in, and if he was humble and asked for help, then he might have the opportunity to study with the other half of the women he was interested in.

When we were finished, the young man could clearly see how studying was going to assist him to fulfill *his* highest values. We linked each of his classes to women (or "chicks," as he liked to put it). Suddenly this young man was inspired to become attentive to all of the things that his father wanted him to master.

He grinned and said, "My therapist didn't teach me this."

Two months passed before I saw him again, and when I did, he told me that his grades had gone up and he'd achieved what he was ultimately after: "scoring with girls." His father approached me, now clearly proud of his son, and wanted to know what I'd done to help spur such incredible scholastic and personal progress in such a short time. I told him what I've revealed throughout this book: all I did with this young man was tap into his specific interests and communicate his father's values in terms of what was truly important to him.

The Power of Communication

Remember that the only thing you can ever rely on or expect people to do consistently is live according to *their* highest values. Mastery in life and in relationships means having the willingness to embrace others for their higher values and uniqueness, not expecting them to change or be more like you. As I've mentioned, within your friendships and family relationships, this is known as *caring*. Outside the circle of those you love, this is called *selling*.

If you're out shopping, for example, and a salesperson approaches you, finds out what you need, and then starts describing a product that's exactly what you've been looking for, don't you open up and become receptive to making a purchase? You immediately want to find out what it does, how much it costs, what other colors it comes in, and so forth. But if the salesperson tries to promote something you're just not interested in, don't you shut down and feel like you want to get away from him or her as soon as possible? You'd prefer to look for what you need elsewhere, rather than having someone try to tell you what you need.

The same principle applies when you're discussing your ideas, skills, products, or even your life purpose with others. When you identify their values and needs and find a way to communicate what you have or want in terms of what's important to them, they open up and become receptive because you care about them.

I'm convinced that there's no such thing as resistant customers or people; they are just individuals expressing their unique hierarchy of values. If you don't connect with and communicate in their highest values, you'll meet resistance—a clue to let you know that you're not connecting and caring. Remember that you "sell" most powerfully when you acknowledge and fulfill the higher values of others.

To sell is not to tell, but to ask instead. When you're in the role of a caring salesperson and you're humble, present, confident, and inspired, you're more likely to ask your potential customers meaningful questions concerning their voids. When you listen attentively, you can easily identify their values and needs because they'll open up and tell you what they really want—in other words, they end up selling themselves.

You become a master of communication, caring, and selling when you're inspired by what you do; you have an attentive look on your face; and you listen carefully, ask questions, and genuinely care about other people's values. In this manner, you also have the greatest potential to find those who will help you fulfill *your* inspired destiny. When your heart is open and you're awake and alive, people will have a natural inclination to want to meet you, be around you, and acquire some part of the energy you possess. When you honor other people's values because they are a reflection of your own, you can truly master the art of communication.

Exercise: Get Inspired!

How to Communicate Using Other People's Values

Try out the following steps to learn how to communicate while consistently tapping into another person's values.

1. Think of something you would love to ask someone to do or give you permission to do. For this example, let's say that you're in high school and want to borrow your father's car so you can visit your friends.

2. What do you think are the top-two values in your father's hierarchy? Write those down. For example, your dad's highest values may be his business and finances. (Remember that other people's lives clearly demonstrate what's most important to them, just as your life demonstrates what's important to you. Think in terms of the seven areas of life: spiritual, mental, vocational, financial, familial, social, and physical.)

3. Come up with at least ten ways in which what you want to do (or have) ties into these two highest values. You could say something like this to your father: "When I borrow the car, I'll have the tire pressure checked and go through the car wash. That will save you time because you won't have to do it before you go to the office on Monday." Or "When I borrow the car, I'll pay for gas and make sure the tank is full when I return it, so you can just get in and drive to the office when you need to."

When you can clearly see how what you'd love to do or have is inspiring and helps fulfill this person's highest values, you increase the probability of him or her being willing to work with you in achieving whatever your outcome may be.

You can apply this process to your family members, friends, colleagues, bosses, significant others, and anyone else you'd like to enhance communication with. When you truly care about people, make sure that you find a way to convey your message (and values) in terms of what's truly meaningful and valuable to them.

Inspired Insights

- Every person has a unique, specific hierarchy of values.

- You have the opposite and complementary values hierarchy to someone else in the world. These opposites often turn up among your family members and other close relationships.

- You view the world through your values, which means that you don't really see the complete picture—when you acknowledge the values of others, however, you expand your perspective.

- *Carelessness* is projecting your values onto other people and trying to change them to become more like you. *Carefulness* is injecting other people's values into your life and trying to change yourself to become more like them.

- Mastering the art of communication means having the ability to be *caring,* both in what is important to you and what is important to another person.

Words of Power

Choose at least one of the following affirmations and repeat it to yourself every day for at least the next month (ideally for the next few months). If this seems particularly challenging (or particularly rewarding), make a commitment to repeat it to yourself every day for the rest of your life.

I take time to discover other people's highest values in life.

*I am a master of communication in my
relationships across all areas of life.*

*I care enough to communicate what is important
to me in terms of what is important to others.*

I honor and appreciate the authentic values of everyone around me.

CHAPTER 6

Making Money Doing What You Love

"Do what you love, the money will follow."
— Marsha Sinetar

What would happen if you could uncover your destiny and then find a way to earn money doing what inspires you? How would you feel if you could make a fortune by pursuing your ultimate life purpose?

Let's take a quick look through history to understand how human beings started dealing with currency in the first place.

The concept of a transaction came about when people began exchanging one thing for another. Inhabitants of ancient civilizations engaged in trading—they used animals, grains, shells, lead, copper, bronze, silver, gold, and other valuable resources to obtain whatever they needed to survive.

Over time, of course, the system evolved, and trading cows turned into trading coins. But as an individual's wealth grew, carrying around a bag of valuable precious metals was no longer feasible and also increased the risk of theft. As a result, trade was conducted with paper money, which (much later) led to the debit and credit cards we use today. And now that we have the Internet, we don't even need to leave our homes to conduct transactions.

What has remained the same is the need for a means of exchange that every person can use and get value from. In whatever form it's in, money is simply the most efficient and effective medium in which to measure any services we have rendered or received.

Every Human Action Can Be Measured in Economics

I've learned that all of us can provide a valuable service. When I had the opportunity to speak at Goodwill Industries International some time ago, I discovered that the company has an amazing attitude toward its employees' abilities. It brings in people off the streets, people who have missing arms and legs, people who are blind, people who are handicapped, and many other people who have some type of mental or physical issue. Instead of robbing these men and women of their dignity, accountability, responsibility, and productivity, this company finds out what their talents are and then puts them to work.

When I arrived to speak at the Goodwill office, I walked into a large room with 75 of the most inspired and productive individuals I had ever met. One person who had no arms was using a mouth-held tool to sort buttons by color, and another was dropping the buttons into some type of size sorter. Others were cutting out usable sections of donated fabric to make quilts. Some were sewing, and some were repairing shoes. My point is that every single employee was contributing, and they were all driven. It was my job to provide an uplifting message, yet *I* was deeply inspired by their "presentation."

No matter what service you'd love to provide for the world, there is a way for you to be paid to do it. *Any service.* To maximize the potential you have to serve from your highest values and be handsomely (or beautifully) paid in return, it's wise to consider transforming what you think about yourself and your financial opportunities.

Start Thinking Like an Entrepreneur

Thinking like an entrepreneur—taking initiative, consciously balancing risk and reward, and managing resources—as early in life as possible will give you a huge advantage in being able to build a great financial fortune doing what you love. This mind-set helps you maximize your time and talent to make a bigger impact on the world.

Let's say, for example, that you're a musician who's in a band with a few friends. Currently, you practice together twice a week in the evenings. About every other weekend, the band plays at a local bar where you're paid per hour for the time you're onstage. These gigs are the band's only source of income for the present moment.

How could you take the band to the next level? And how else might you get paid for the value you provide? To start, in addition to your hourly rate for performances, you could book new venues where you'd also charge people at the door. And to bring in a larger audience, you could distribute flyers and send e-mails to all of your friends and family letting them know the upcoming dates you'll be playing. In this manner, you're using your time and networks much more efficiently.

While you're performing, you could record the show and then sell the CDs, or you could give them away to generate even more interest. You might think about creating a product or promotional tool for your band as well. You could, for example, set up a Website with an online store for customers to buy your CDs or download digital files. This is where you'd start to generate some revenue without needing your physical presence to make it happen. Having a continually increasing fan base (driven by word of mouth and access to your music even when you're not performing) could also provide an incentive for every band member to take his or her musical skills to the next level.

By thinking like an entrepreneur and treating your band like an innovative business model, you'd be doing almost exactly the same thing as you were previously when you were earning only on a time-for-money basis, except you'd be utilizing your resources to increase not only your income but also your social recognition and status.

Here's another scenario: Let's say you're currently a student. What are the possibilities? When I was attending the University of Houston, I used to tutor. And when I was in graduate school, I used to "present" classes six or seven nights a week, teaching whatever I had learned earlier that day. This helped me pay for most of my education. I made enough money to cover my accommodations, textbooks, and study resources—almost everything I needed! The opportunity I created also made me more self-confident and taught me how to promote myself, which has no doubt assisted me in building the recognition that I have today.

Perhaps you'll decide to start tutoring other students in your own classes, and help them understand the topics that you've already mastered. But let's take it a step further. Why not tutor more than one student at a time and perhaps form a group? Why not tutor online, offering your services to people who aren't even on the same campus as you? You'd be spending the same amount of time teaching, except you'd be making ten (or more) times the income than you would if you were tutoring just one student.

You could also write an article about one of your classes that gets sent out to the student body. By stepping up and having a say, you would be building recognition for yourself and would probably gain even more students as a result. Once you started making a substantial income, you'd find that this would give you incentive to study harder and focus on mastering your classes so that you could continue teaching. Not only would you be mastering your courses, but you'd also get ahead in your career by gaining valuable work experience. Remember that you learn what you teach the most.

Many people assume that while they're in school, they don't have time to earn extra money. When you start thinking like an entrepreneur, however, you realize that there are no limits to what you can do. You may as well take advantage of whatever time and energy you have throughout your life to serve others and get richly rewarded while doing so. *You deserve it!*

Maybe you appreciate this concept but worry about having to "sell stuff." That may be because you have this old belief that all selling is like pushing used cars onto unsuspecting customers or convincing people to buy things they don't really need. But the truth is that nothing happens or gets done in the world until someone "sells" something to someone, whether it's a tangible thing or an idea. Selling is what prompts any kind of exchange; and the greatest type is about fair exchange, trading value for commensurate value.

No matter where you are today, if you start to think outside the box and associate with individuals who think globally, you'll begin to see new and greater possibilities for yourself. You really can do what you love when you have the vision, inspiration, and purpose to achieve it. In fact, the greater your goal is, the more resources you'll attract to fulfill that inspired dream.

What Would You Do with $5 Million?

Many years ago, I interviewed a gentleman who applied for a job as a manager with my company. He walked into my office with a smile on his face, and he seemed like a very intelligent guy. He shook my hand, looked me in the eyes, and said he knew that he was the right person for the job and appreciated the opportunity to apply for the position.

We both sat down and I asked, "If I gave you a check for $5 million right now, what would you do with it?" And right there on the spot, I took out my checkbook and started writing his name on a check. (If you were at an interview and your potential employer was all of a sudden writing you a multimillion-dollar check, what would be going through your mind?)

I filled it out, held it up, and asked him to check the spelling of his name. The guy looked at the check, then at me, and then back at the check. He didn't know what to say.

I wanted to know what he'd do if I gave him the money, so I said, "It's $5 million. If I gave you this, perhaps you'd never have to work another day in your life. What would you do?"

The man leaned back in his chair and relaxed. His façade was gone. "Well, if I didn't have to work and I had all the money I needed, I would focus on my hobbies." I asked him what type of things he loved doing, and he replied that he loved woodworking the most, and if he was wealthy, he would make furniture by hand and spend all day at his woodworking shop.

After listening to his answer, I stood up. "Thank you. That will be all."

He got up slowly. "Is the interview over?"

I told him it was.

"Did I get the position?"

"No, you didn't."

"Is there a specific reason, Dr. Demartini? Do you mind if I ask what made you decide so quickly?"

"It's very simple. I'm hiring for a management position, and you just said that if you didn't have to work another day in your life, you would be making furniture. If you have such great management skills, why haven't you managed your life so that you're doing something you really love? Why would I hire you if you haven't figured out how to manage your own life?"

Nodding, the man replied, "Wow, I can't argue with that. That's a powerful question." So he shook my hand, probably feeling a little down and shocked but definitely thoughtful, and he disappeared.

Three weeks later, I was in my office and the man came to visit me. He arrived with a large brown paper bag and sat down in the same chair he'd taken during the interview. I also sat down in the same place, and he said, "Dr. Demartini, I just want to thank you."

"Why is that?"

"Because what you said to me a few weeks ago was just about the most amazing thing I'd ever heard, and it absolutely changed my life. After looking for a job for three months, it finally occurred to me: why don't I just do what I love and figure out a way to earn a living from it? So, I'm now in business for myself, making my own furniture. Thank you for asking me that question. It's true: if I'm really that great at managing, then why not start managing my life the way I really want it to be?"

Then he picked up the bag and presented me with some beautiful handmade tissue-box holders that matched the wood in my office.

When you aren't inspired by what you do and don't love your career, you cost the company you're working for (as well as yourself) a fortune. On the other hand, you increase the probability of being rewarded financially when you can't wait to get up in the morning to do what you do. Finding what you're inspired by and determining a way to turn that into a service for other people is an extremely valuable investment.

Exercise: Get Inspired!

How to Find Your Inspired Service

1. Examine your hierarchy of values, and think about the areas where you feel most empowered. Write down the top three. (For example, your top-three values may be family, fitness/health, and nature/beauty.)

2. Now think about the services you've already provided for people around you. (For example, you may jot down something like this: "I helped my sister move into her new house. I helped my son's coach drive the soccer team to the league finals. I helped pick up litter at the park.")

3. Write down a list of all of your skills, assets, and talents that would be valuable to provide for others as a service. (Perhaps your skills are that you're a fast reader, excellent at math, a great team player, and so on; your assets are your physical strength and endurance, intelligence, compassion, and so on; and your talents are that you're a fast runner, an agile soccer player, a good singer, and so on.)

4. From the list that you've created from the previous step, circle the things that are most inspiring to you and that you'd love to do for others.

5. Ask yourself, *Whom could I provide this service to, and who would love to pay me in return?*

6. Identify the individuals or groups who would benefit from your skills and talents.

What could you do with the talents, assets, and skills listed above? How might this be turned into a service for others? Maybe it would be running a soccer program for younger kids, teaching at a fitness camp, or tutoring students in reading and math. Or perhaps it could be helping families to start exercising together. The possibilities just keep coming as you list more and more of what you love.

As you consider whom you might serve, be sure to think about the people in your immediate environment and what they may need. But don't stop there—expand your thinking to your whole town, city, state, and even your nation (and perhaps beyond to other countries). There are no limits to how much of an impact you can make doing what you love, particularly when you embody the powerful principle of fair exchange into every act of service.

The Power of Fair Exchange

It's wise to maintain an equal exchange when you're being compensated to do what you love—that is, to give and receive fairly and ensure that both your needs and the needs of those you serve are being met. Anytime you're able to maintain fair exchange when you're providing a service to others, you dissolve any emotions of fear and guilt (and other distractions) that might otherwise get in the way, and you become grateful for the opportunity to serve and be rewarded.

You might believe that making money by doing what you love and fulfilling your purpose in life means that someone else will lose out financially. Or perhaps you believe that you'll be losing out financially (or in some other way) whenever other people are rewarded for doing what they love. Yet it's beneficial to balance your own interests and importance with what's important to and interesting for others. This brings your service and reward into a powerful, fair exchange; thereby, you consciously align with the Universal Laws—you tap into the hidden power that exists in the Universe.

Fair exchange helps you accumulate wealth faster than *unfair* exchange. Unfair exchange is charging too much for too little service or undervaluing yourself and not charging what you're worth. When you don't consciously make the effort to deal in fair exchange, you accumulate a long list of all your imbalanced transactions, which then holds you back from being focused and present in the areas of life that are important to you. This generates negative emotions that distract you from achieving your inspired dreams. When you maintain an equal exchange, however, you consistently value yourself, your time, and your service for what they're worth—even as you value other people, their time, and their service for what *they* are worth.

People love to be recognized when they provide a service, and fair exchange is a simple way to do it. Fair exchange has the power to move people, and these expressions of gratitude between you and those you serve can open up communication and cooperation with anyone in your life. It could be your boss, employee, friend, neighbor, sibling, partner, and so on. Every person responds to gratitude.

This principle is so profound that it even helps you bring people back into your life or let both of you move on separately to a higher ground of living and accomplishment. Keeping your service balanced is a vital technique to increase your material and mental value. Make the conscious effort to be in fair exchange throughout your life—no matter whom you're serving or what service you're providing—and you'll continually increase your value to you and the world.

Your Value to the World

When you fulfill your own voids and values, you become valuable to yourself. When you fulfill the voids of others, you become valuable to them. Whenever you study your habits and apply the principles and methods of personal development, you grow your own self-worth and expand your potential and awareness, which makes you more valuable to society. Doing business is simply the act of fulfilling other people's values and receiving financial reward in return.

You have the capacity to offer astounding value to other people in any of the seven areas of life where your inspired destiny lies. Anything that can satisfy a person's void is an opportunity for you to make money doing what you love. As I've mentioned, money is simply the most effective and efficient vehicle of exchange when being rewarded for providing a service. It's important to know that money goes where it's appreciated most. So if you act on the opportunities you have, then it's almost impossible for you not to earn an income while fulfilling your destiny.

Remember that your value in society is equivalent to how many problems you can solve, how many questions you can answer, and how many voids you can fill with your services or products. Those who amass substantial wealth are the ones who have figured out a way to serve the greatest number of people on the largest scale with something that is absolutely inspiring. Take Bill Gates—he is a multibillionaire because he created a product that benefits countless individuals. His mission was to have a computer in every single household around the world—and if you deliver something that everyone can benefit from, then there's no way you won't be successful. You are almost guaranteed to build a fortune doing what you love.

Like many men and women, you may be living in fear instead of moving forward with inspiration and purpose. Instead of living your dreams and finding ways to serve others while doing so, you may be letting anxiety cloud the truth of what you'd love to do. Beware: when you're thinking only about yourself, you're bound to live in fear. As soon as you start focusing equally on others, you move beyond yourself and realize that there's nothing to be afraid of. People just want to be cared for and made to feel special and appreciated when you're serving them by doing what you love.

In addition to recognizing the incredible value that sits inside your inspired service for humanity, it is also wise to acknowledge the great wealth you already have.

You Already Have a Vast Fortune

You, like everyone else in the world, already possess a vast fortune. It's what allows you to be financially compensated for the services you provide. Although you may not acknowledge this, it isn't missing from your life—your riches are just in a form that you don't or can't currently recognize.

If, for example, your mental area of life is a high value, then your wealth is in the form of ideas, research, intellect, knowledge, and insights into different topics or disciplines. If your physical area of life is a high value, then your beauty, muscle tone, flexibility, or endurance might be your form of wealth. If your social and family areas are high values, then your wealth may be the relationships and experiences with your family members or others who spend time with you. Your fortune is always conserved within your highest values and the areas in your life where you're most focused and disciplined.

I once knew a socialite who was somewhat impoverished financially. She owned one nice outfit that she wore every time she attended parties and gatherings. When you met her, you'd get the impression that she was relatively wealthy just by her appearance (unless you happened to see her at more than one event). Despite her situation, she introduced herself and made connections with some of the real movers and shakers in America.

After she confessed to me that she struggled with money, I told her, "You make contacts so easily with amazing people. You know them, you talk to them, and you're in their circle of influence. But you don't value yourself 'cash-wise.'" This woman was gifted with networking, but she just hadn't taken the time to appreciate and take advantage of the financial opportunities that were available to her.

I asked, "What would happen if you introduced yourself to CEOs and then connected them with other people you know who could do business with them, and then took a cut of the deal?"

"Oh! Do you think people would mind?"

"If you're helping them make millions of dollars, then *no*, I don't think they'd object." So I helped her create a company based on the service of connecting influential people. This woman's role (what she already loved to do and was naturally good at) was to attend functions, socialize, and make contacts. She'd also keep a record of individuals' needs and what they were looking for, and when she made successful connections, she would have her clients sign a document saying that if they conducted any business transactions, she would be given a percentage of it. This lady recognized her inner fortune and created a highly valuable service for others. This way, she was doing what she loved and making millions doing it. She overcame her prior challenges and was able to lead a very fulfilling, satisfying life.

Exercise: Get Inspired!

Discover Your Wealth

1. Write down 300 ways in which you're already wealthy in life. (For example, you could write: "I'm wealthy in knowledge about my family history, my physical appearance, my ability to speak and inspire others, and my athletic skills that come naturally.")

2. Think about the resources you've identified. Have you ever acknowledged them before? Take time now to reflect on the hidden riches within your highest values. Realize that your wealth is simply in a form that you might not have recognized, and become inspired and grateful for your unique, vast fortune.

Get Paid While Pursuing What You Love

When you truly care about others and serve them by honoring their hierarchy of values, the doors of opportunity will keep opening for you. A vast number of jobs become available when you're inspired and enthusiastic about what you do. Consciously put yourself in environments where you can provide your service and develop new ways to do what you love and be fairly compensated for it.

Overcome your fears about being rejected or not having enough money, and ask around if there's anyone you can provide your services to. Your genuine inspiration will be your biggest selling point. People want to work with those who are vibrant and love what they do, and they'll be more than happy to pay for it.

Look at any job on the planet, and you'll find that it provides something that is "missing." Every job provides a solution, answers a mystery, or fills a void with a value. No matter what it is that you'd love to do, there's a niche for it and a group of people who would benefit from your service.

Inspired Insights

- Every human action can be measured economically. No matter what it is that you'd love to do, there's a way for you to get rewarded financially by providing that service.

- Your inspired service to the world comes out of your highest values in life.

- The more challenges you tackle, the more problems you solve, the more mysteries you unravel, and the more questions you answer through your service, the more valuable you will be to the world.

- Maintaining fair exchange is the fuel that increases your acts of service to the world and keeps you out of cycles of unfair exchange.

- You already have a vast fortune; it resides within your highest values.

Words of Power

Choose at least one of the following affirmations and repeat it to yourself every day for at least the next month (ideally for the next few months). If this seems particularly challenging (or particularly rewarding), make a commitment to repeat it to yourself every day for the rest of your life.

I do what I love, I love what I do, and I am paid well to do it.

My payments are due when my services are rendered, and I stay in fair exchange.

I pay myself first, for I am worthy of it.

I am always in the right place at the right time to meet the right person to make the right deal.

CHAPTER 7

Overcoming the Seven Fears and Living Purposefully

*"You can conquer almost any fear if you will only
make up your mind to do so. For remember, fear
doesn't exist anywhere except in the mind."*
— Dale Carnegie

Deep inside your heart, you know what you would love to be doing with your life. You're aware of your highest values and wish to pursue an inspired existence. Still, there are seven primary fears that can hold you back and immobilize you, keeping you from realizing the ways in which you're already expressing your highest values. These fears correlate directly to the seven areas of life (spiritual, mental, vocational, financial, familial, social, and physical). As you read this chapter, take a moment to consider which ones are currently preventing you from discovering your inspired destiny.

1. The Fear of Going Against a Spiritual Authority

Some people worry about challenging the morals or ethics of a religious institution or so-called spiritual authority figure and perceive their life purpose as "not good enough," "too worldly," "self-centered," or even "unholy." So they try to forget their calling and pursue something that's more aligned with the values of their place of worship or their family's religious tradition.

Do you think this makes them more spiritual when they sacrifice what they love for what they think they should do? No, it doesn't. But it's also a trick question because it doesn't make them less spiritual, either. Know this: all of us are inspired or spiritual regardless of how we express ourselves. No one is more or less spiritual than anyone else. To make comparisons doesn't reflect the genuine nature of spirituality.

Maybe you've been on the receiving end of this kind of judgment, with individuals telling you that you're "less spiritual" because you've chosen a particular path. Realize that this is a projection of their values, an expectation for you to live according to *their* hierarchy. The truth is that you're needed in the world exactly as you are. Whatever you're *inspired* by in life is your unique expression of spirituality.

Someone who is dedicated to raising a family will believe that his or her spiritual quest is parenting. Entrepreneurs will see that their mission is to build successful businesses, and that is also a spiritual path. Those who are involved in government and participate in social causes will see this as their spiritual path. Someone who wants to succeed in property development views that as a spiritual purpose. Albert Einstein asserted that if the Divine is omnipresent, omniscient, and omnipotent, then every experience, action, and aspiration of human beings must also be part of that spiritual path.

Sometimes you submit to outside influences and inject those values into your life, and then you become afraid of crossing or challenging them. **Ultimately, your only spiritual authority is your own higher being, or what some have called your *inner soul*.** It's interesting to note that many of the leaders of the great spiritual traditions followed their inner knowing, even if it meant parting ways with current beliefs or traditions of the times. In some cases, defying convention actually helped them initiate their own new spiritual practices.

2. The Fear of Not Being Smart Enough

You may believe that you don't have the mental acuity to fulfill your purpose in life. If so, this is often due to subordination to an external authority or a comparison to someone who you think possesses more knowledge, creativity, imagination, or education than you do. Whenever you're convinced that another person is above you or somehow better than you, you put him or her on a pedestal while minimizing yourself.

I wasn't able to read a book from cover to cover until I was almost 18. I gradually overcame my dyslexia and did learn how to read, write, and communicate quite well. Yet for years, I was intimidated by intelligent people—that is, until my own vocabulary began to grow and my confidence in reading and learning accelerated.

The truth is that you have a Ph.D. equivalent in your own life. In other words, no one knows as much as you do about your life and your inspired destiny. Nobody has more authority on the topic of your purpose than you do. It's unwise to feel inferior to someone just because he or she possesses a great mind. Even Sir Isaac Newton once said, "If I have seen further than other men it is because I have stood on the shoulders of giants." So stand on the shoulders of those *you* admire instead of groveling at their feet, and give yourself permission to do something extraordinary with your own mind.

It's important to know that every human being has every trait, so we must look inside and figure out where we have whatever we perceive "they" have. In essence, at the level of the soul we are all the same; it's in our physical existence where we are individuals with our own hierarchy of values.

Your values are what make your identity unique, even though you possess every trait and characteristic a human can have.

Nothing is missing! When you notice that someone has a sharp intellect, ask yourself where you also display this, and don't stop until you awaken your full awareness of it.

You have the greatest mental capacities in the areas of life that are highest on your hierarchy of values. Feeling inferior shrinks you and prevents you from discovering your hidden genius. The truth is that you have a great mind, too, so instead of minimizing yourself, ask yourself, *Where do I equally demonstrate greatness of mind, and what is the next biggest horizon I can aim for now?*

3. The Fear of Failing

Imagine that you're a toddler trying to walk for the first time. As you attempt to take steps, you fall down quite a bit. What do you say to yourself? *I'm a failure?!* No. It's more probable that you're thinking something like this: *Better try that again.* If your vision is to walk, then you're going to get back up, no matter how many times you fall.

When you think you're a failure, what's actually going on is that you're being tested to see if you're setting goals that are in harmony with your higher values. If you're not really committed to a goal, you'll let the perception of failure stop you from going forward. You'll either readjust and move on to something that's more inspiring, or you'll set unrealistic expectations and create fantasies about who you are and what you're supposed to do (and keep setting yourself up for more perceived failures). If you set goals that align with your higher values and purpose, then you won't give up until you achieve your destiny. Both failure and success are nothing more than "feedback systems" that ensure that your objectives are authentic and express your highest values.

When you're clear about your objectives and they're in alignment with your highest values, you'll do whatever it takes, travel whatever distance, and pay whatever price to achieve them. You'll embrace pain and pleasure, support and challenge, and anything else the Universe presents in the pursuit of your inspired purpose.

Almost everyone has experienced momentary flashes of success and failure along the journey of life. The second you think you're successful, you're often on your way down; the second you feel you're failing, you're usually on your way up. Misguided perceptions or exaggerations of failure can wake you up and get you back to focusing on the high-priority actions to achieve your desired outcome. The same inaccurate view of success can make you inflexible and throw you off track. Moreover, according to Don Keough, the former president of Coca-Cola, the knowledge of failure can lead to success: "I have always been afraid of the word success. People, companies and countries can get into trouble when they start to think they're successful. They get arrogant."

Like Keough, I'm not interested in momentary feelings of success. I'm interested in living a meaningful life. These feelings are opposites that are your constant companions as you follow your inspired path. If you have time to be worried about success and failure, this is an indicator that you've distracted yourself from the actual service you're here to provide. This happens when you're focused more on yourself and your emotions instead of maintaining a healthy balance between yourself and your service to others. It's unlikely to feel like a success or a failure when you're present and dedicated to a purpose greater than your own immediate needs.

4. The Fear of Losing or Not Making Money

Some people worry that they might not make enough to support themselves while doing what they love, or they're afraid of losing what they do have while pursuing their mission. Yet it's nearly impossible not to make money if you're dedicated to a cause of service bigger than yourself, and your higher values include saving and investing. Remember that one of the keys to building wealth is communicating what you'd love to do in terms of other people's values. When you care about their needs and maintain a fair exchange, you'll have no trouble earning an income.

As I've mentioned, one of the greatest things you can ever do is learn how to create fair exchange. Give the people around you way more than they expect, and then charge a fair price. When you put this into practice, you'll realize that there's never a lack of money in the world; there's only an unwillingness to search for ways to provide your service to others in a manner that fills their needs.

Saving and investing are powerful ways to help you quickly overcome your fears regarding finances. When you pay yourself first (and invest in yourself), your wealth accelerates. By doing this, you gradually release your focus on loss or lack.

Know that whenever you're overwhelmed by your fear, your mind is clouded and you make unwise decisions. On the other hand, when you're poised and balanced and have created sound financial strategies, you make wise decisions. Remember that people love to engage with you when you're inspired by what you do, and you honor your highest values.

5. *The Fear of Angering Your Loved Ones or Losing Their Respect*

What would happen if you were to tell your loved ones what you *really* want to do with your life? How would they react, and how much does their opinion matter? Do you worry that if you revealed your inspired purpose, you'd lose the respect of (or perhaps even be rejected by) the people who are most important to you?

Many years ago, I met a man who was struggling with his new business. Whatever profit he earned, he was sending most of it to his family in Japan. Meanwhile, he and his wife and baby were living on almost nothing, but this man's pride and fear of losing his parents' respect had him handing over about 60 percent of his income. He was afraid to tell his mother and father the truth, even though his own family was living on rice and beans. When his wife finally insisted that they could no longer live this way, the man came to me and asked for my advice.

In turn, I asked him, "If your parents knew what was going on, do you really think they would want you to sacrifice your family for them?"

He replied that he wasn't sure what they'd want.

So I probed deeper. "I think you're caught in this cultural idealism instead of what's real in this moment," I observed. "The wisest thing to do is to tell your parents the truth and redistribute the wealth, and then get on with serving people and growing your business. When your company is bringing in more revenue and you want to start sending money to your parents again, then do so, but keep your priorities in order. Remember that your wife and baby are wisely your highest priorities right now."

The man agreed and told his parents what he'd decided with new courage. He humbled himself, and as soon as he was finished talking, both his mother and father insisted that he not send them anything until he got on his feet. Once he unloaded himself of all that pressure and stress, he was able to focus on his business plan and achieve tremendous success.

When you're doing what you love and following your inspired destiny, it doesn't mean that you don't want to help the people you love. It's not wise, however, to sacrifice yourself for what loved ones *might* think and let it interfere with what you are actually here to do. Whenever you give up or put aside your hierarchy of values for someone else's, you'll automatically feel frustrated and resentful because you're not being true to yourself. Finding a balance and creating a fair exchange between yourself and others is the key to achieving your inspired destiny.

6. The Fear of Rejection

Let me just lay it out: It's impossible to go through life without having other people feel irritated with you. You can't please everyone all the time. Heck, you can't even please yourself more than half the time! So, you can't expect all those you cross paths with to have (or like) the same values as you do.

A perfect balance of opposites—rejection and acceptance—will exist no matter where you are or in what stage of life you find yourself. Acknowledging this will free you up from overreaction. For example, whenever I get a standing ovation for a speech or presentation, I *could* start thinking that everyone agrees with me and accepts what I've said as the best thing they've ever heard. I *could* start getting a lopsided (and inaccurate) view of who I am and how I interact with others. But I know that the perfect balance will always be there, so I can see that half the people are standing because they're genuinely inspired, and the other half are standing either because they're glad it's time to leave or they don't want to stand out from the rest of the crowd.

Similarly, if you can see that what appears to be rejection is only *half* of your reality and acceptance is the other half, you can free yourself from overreacting whenever you perceive some type of rejection in life. You also accelerate your growth and empower yourself when you can embrace the reality that at times you'll be perceived as the cause of pleasure *and* pain in the people around you.

How can you deal with rejection when it looks like that's what you'll get if you do what you love? Here's what I do: If I have a seemingly nonnegotiable choice between pissing others off or myself, I choose to piss others off because I would rather stay true to myself and follow my heart. (I call this the "Law of the Lesser Pissers.") I learned a long time ago that I would rather the whole world be against me than my own soul. I realize that I can't please everybody, and when I go out there and speak, I'll receive praise *and* criticism. This doesn't mean that I don't consider and respect other people's values—rather, it just means that since there are complementary opposite values in the world, I'm certain to displease some as I please others.

If you're afraid of expressing your truth because you're worried about what someone else will think of you, you block yourself from sharing the greatest gift of your heart. Instead, be willing to do your best to communicate your vision in terms of other people's values, and know that since everyone has a different set of values, it will be impossible for you to reach some type of consensus. It's wise for you to embrace both aspects. Hold on to your purpose regardless of the responses you may receive, and maintain the vision of your inspired destiny.

Remember that in the moment when somebody is challenging or criticizing you, another person is supporting or praising you. If you pay attention, you'll find this balance in every interaction. You'll never experience rejection without some kind of acceptance as well. Look for both occurring in the same moment; and you'll be poised, present, and powerful. You won't be distracted by fear or guilt.

Know that **all fears are an illusion.** The word *fear* stands for False Evidence Appearing Real. It's an assumption that you're going to experience more challenge than support, more pain than pleasure, or more loss than gain at some point in the future. In truth, you won't receive that because with every crisis, there's a blessing. For every negative, there's a positive. The two sides of life are always present.

7. The Fear of Not Being Physically Attractive or Having Enough Vitality

Are you afraid that you don't have the right "look" to achieve your dream? Perhaps you allow your imbalanced perspective on your appearance to stop you from going after what's most important to you, and you shrink yourself instead of growing to reach your higher potential.

You might not love certain parts of your body and wish they were different. If that's true, take time to ask yourself how every single body part helps you fulfill your destiny: *How do my hands assist me to achieve my purpose? How do my legs assist me to achieve my purpose?* Ask yourself over and over until you're grateful for your body as it is and until you can clearly see how all parts are assisting you to achieve your dream.

Thinking that you're "too young" or "too old" is another aspect of this fear. Instead of getting locked into the idea of a "perfect age" for realizing your dreams, bring the value and wisdom of youth or the experience of your years of life to the people you touch with your inspired service of love. You're never too young or too old to discover your purpose and work toward fulfilling it.

If you're afraid of not having enough physical energy to complete your objectives and live out your dream, remember that when you do what you love and you love what you do, you have more energy that will constantly fuel you. Whenever people ask me where I get all of my energy, I tell them it's because I love what I do, I do what I love every day, and I'm clear about where I'm headed.

So take time and make a real effort to become crystal clear on your purpose and where you're going. I call this "Master-Planning for Life." If you have a detailed road map, it's so much easier to get where you'd really love to go.

Don't Let Your Fears Stop You from Living a Magnificent Life

So perhaps you worry that you'll overstep the moral boundaries or ethics of some spiritual authority or that you don't possess the intelligence to achieve your dreams. You may fear that you'd fail at fulfilling your purpose or that you'd lose money (or not make any) just by doing what you love. You might be afraid that your loved ones will leave you or not accept what you know is your destiny. You may be concerned that you'll face tons of rejection and lose your friends. And perhaps you fret that you don't have the body or the energy required to create the life you desire.

Each of these fears clouds your mind and obscures the sunny truth that sits inside your heart: *You are destined to shine and touch the lives of others.* Remember that deep within, you know what you would truly love to do with your life.

Inspired Insights

- The seven primary fears may be holding you back and preventing you from openly and consciously expressing what you are most inspired to do.

- Your fears can compound and stop you from taking action toward creating an extraordinary life.

- It's wise to set yourself free of your present fears so that you may live a magnificent, inspiring life.

Words of Power

Choose at least one of the following affirmations and repeat it to yourself every day for at least the next month (ideally for the next few months). If this seems particularly challenging (or particularly rewarding), make a commitment to repeat it to yourself every day for the rest of your life.

I break through my fears and pursue what I love in life.

Every part of my being helps me achieve my life's purpose.

I am destined to shine and touch the lives of others.

I have within me everything I need to fulfill my highest values.

CHAPTER 8

The Keys to Mastering Your Life

"One can never consent to creep when one feels an impulse to soar."
— **Helen Keller**

Henry Ford once said, "Whether you think you can or think you can't, you're right." If that's true, what do you think is the difference between "I can" and "I can't"? I contend whenever you set goals for yourself that align with your highest values, you build confidence. You end up believing "I am" in your being, "I know" in your senses, and "I can" in your physical motor functions.

But when you set goals that aren't aligned with your highest values, you diminish your confidence. You end up believing "I'm not" in your being, "I don't know" in your senses, and "I can't" in your physical motor functions. You start to doubt yourself and feel inferior, injecting other people's values into your life. Every time you live with an "I can't" belief, you blur your inspired vision, making it more difficult to stay focused on what you love.

It's vital to realize that you increase your self-worth every time you set a goal that's important to you. Upon building your confidence and an "I can" belief in yourself, you'll awaken your authentic sense of leadership, which already exists within you. You become more reliable because you're dedicated, focused, and organized. People will trust you and be inspired by your example. Developing a sense of "I can" about who you are and what you're capable of makes it possible for you to take advantage of every opportunity for career advancement, attract the relationships you'd love to have, and generate the income you'd love to earn.

I am certain that it's my destiny to fulfill my mission. When you recognize and harmonize with your highest values, you'll have that kind of certainty, too. You create that authentic confidence in your areas of highest value. This is where you concentrate the most and where you seek to have the most mastery. You're dedicated to learning what most inspires you or what's highest on your list of values, and you'll be disciplined to attain any necessary skills. Ensure that you set your goals and objectives to align with your highest values, and there are no limits to what you can achieve.

The Truth about Low Self-Esteem

While working with thousands of people from all over the world who believe that their low self-esteem is what holds them back from discovering and pursuing their purpose in life, I discovered something: Their lack of confidence relates to—you guessed it!—their hierarchy of values. It's an indicator that they're directing their focus and actions on something that is lower on their values list.

All human beings feel self-assured when they're acting in accordance to their highest values and will experience low self-esteem when they act according to their lowest values. Therefore, you're going to have low self-esteem in the areas of life that relate to your lowest values and simultaneously have high self-esteem in the areas that relate to your highest values. Your overall self-worth is the balance between these two aspects.

Here's a quick example that illustrates my point: When I had the opportunity to speak to about 200 people outside of New York City in 2007, a woman in the audience asked, "Dr. Demartini, what do you do when you have a 12-year-old who has low self-esteem, learning problems, and zero motivation?"

I walked over to this woman's son and asked if he had just heard what his mother said. (Yes, he had.) "Do you beat yourself up about that?" (Of course he did.)

I looked him in the eyes, smiled, and said, "So, where do you shine? Where do you think you're smarter, more skilled, and more confident than anyone else? Where do you think you're the most brilliant? What area of life is it in?"

His answer came quickly. "Playing video games!"

Then I asked what type of games he likes and how he compares to his friends' playing skills. He told me that ice hockey is his favorite and that he beats his friends at it all the time.

"Stand up and tell me about this ice-hockey video game," I requested. And right there, in front of 200 people, this young boy stood and recited almost all of the famous names in hockey. He also revealed his strategies and what moves he makes to win.

His mother looked astonished as she watched how outgoing her son had just become, and how clear, sharp, and articulate he was. All I did was ask him questions that were aligned to his highest values in life. This youngster had an astounding photographic memory of the video game, and I could tell that the rest of the people in the audience were ready to applaud him. I continued asking questions and found out what class he was struggling with the most (math) and then showed him the connection between it and his highest values, linking schoolwork to what he loved doing (just as I had done with the 19-year-old student who loved "chicks").

Soon enough, he could clearly see how studying math was going to assist him in being a higher achiever in ice-hockey video games. After just 14 minutes of linking his math class to his highest values, the boy turned to his mother and asked, "Can you get me that math book that will help me with ice hockey?"

Smiling, his mother wiped a tear from her cheek, and the entire audience sat there with a collective "Wow!" on their lips.

You Are Already Successful

A gentleman once came to me for a consultation and said, "I feel like I'm a failure, and I want to be more successful."

I asked him to start naming what areas of life he was already successful in, but he insisted that he was *not* successful. So I asked again.

"I don't think you're hearing me," the man replied.

"Okay. So where are you successful already?"

The man took a deep breath. "We aren't getting off to a good start, Dr. Demartini. I said that I'm *not* successful, and I want to *be* successful."

"Think about what I'm saying—I'm being sincere. My certainty exceeds your doubt. I know in my heart that you *are* already successful. So let's take a look at the areas of life where you've demonstrated this."

This time he made an effort and reflected for a while before answering. He mentioned that he had a wonderful relationship with his wife, with whom he'd been married for almost 20 years. Halfheartedly, he added. "I guess I have 'success' there."

"Absolutely. Where else?"

Still somewhat pained by my question, he searched his heart again. "Well, now that I think about it, my son and I are pretty successful. He plays baseball, and I coach his team—we may go undefeated this year . . . so, we're definitely doing well there."

"That's a success, isn't it?" He agreed that it was. "Keep going," I urged him.

Now he was really in the flow and said, "Well, my wife's mother lives with us, and most people don't get along with their in-laws, but she and I have a very close bond. She's like my second mother. So we have a successful relationship, too."

This time I just nodded, as he didn't need more prodding from me.

"You know where else I'm successful? My family and I have been planting lots of flowers, and we might win a 'Yard of the Month' award in our neighborhood. And another thing: I've never thought about this, but I'm also a lay minister at my church. I lead a prayer group on Wednesdays, and sometimes on Sundays I step up to preach. I guess that I do have some areas that are successful."

Finally, he was beginning to see that he was successful in many areas of his life, and now that we were on the same page, I explained, "For you to label yourself a 'failure,' you must be comparing yourself to someone you think is more successful. Is this accurate?"

"Well, there's a doctor who lives up the hill from me. He makes more money than I do and owns a bigger home."

"Does this man have a strong relationship with a significant other, like the one you have with your wife? Or with his child or mother-in-law? Does he have a fulfilling role like yours at your church?"

The man frowned, saying, "Oh, no—not at all. Unfortunately, none of those things is going well for him."

"Would you trade places with him? If not, perhaps you've just been trying to be someone you aren't instead of appreciating yourself the way you are."

After a few more minutes of talking about this, the man discovered that his achievements could be found in areas that related to *his* highest values in life and that he wouldn't sacrifice his forms of success for his neighbor's (or anyone else's). When we were finished, he had tears in his eyes as he recognized what magnificent success he had already achieved in his life.

Remember that no one in the world has the exact same hierarchy of values as you do. Your highest values determine your purpose, and they also determine your form of success, which I prefer to simply call your areas of greatest achievement. You create your life according to your hierarchy, so it's essential to honor the accomplishments that reflect your highest values instead of comparing yourself to others.

No one experiences more successes than failures, or vice versa. Michael Jordan once said, "If I am more successful than most people, it is because I had more [so-called] failures than most people." When you're aligned with your highest values, there's no competition with anyone else because your values are what make your life goals unique. When you're true to yourself, your heart guides your decisions, and you'll be firmly on the path toward your inspired destiny.

Exercise: Get Inspired!

Find Your Success in Life

1. Make a list of your accomplishments and the areas in which you feel that you're achieving the most out of life.

2. While you're making the list, focus on the specific items that brought you the greatest fulfillment and were the most inspiring.

3. Examine your hierarchy of values, and note how your successes reflect your highest values.

The truth is that you'll have mastery in the areas of life that have the greatest importance to you, and it's nearly impossible for you to ever miss a beat in making sure that your highest values are being fulfilled with great success.

Moving Forward and Pursuing Your Purpose

The Delphic oracle advised: "Know thyself, be thyself, love thyself." You would be wise to heed this, too: Being attuned to your authentic self and your highest values is crucial for a magnificent, inspired life. This is the difference between becoming a powerful leader or a disempowered follower. It's the difference that determines what kind of career you'll have, what kind of relationships you'll create, what level of income you'll earn, and what you feel you're truly worthy of receiving.

Knowing yourself allows you to target your profession or field of choice, get clear on your dream and future, tap into your genius and unlock your talents in life, become sharp and focused on your mission, and open the door to incredible physical energy and vitality. The more you're aware of your highest and most authentic values, the more you'll honor yourself as you are instead of trying to change or disown parts of yourself to be like someone else.

You have two choices: You can identify what's truly important to you in life and set your goals and dreams to be in alignment with your values, or you can sit back and see what the world has to offer you. You can live "from cause" or "at effect." Living from cause means that you're the one who chooses your destiny and you're the catalyst for all events that occur in your life. On the other hand, living at effect means that you allow your reactive emotions and the opinions of those around you to dictate your journey through life.

Count your blessings daily and foster deep appreciation for who you are, your highest values, and the areas where you feel most confident. Acknowledge that you are worthy, and what you'd love to do does indeed provide incredible value for other people. Ask yourself every day: *What would I really love to do, and how can I be handsomely or beautifully paid to do what most inspires me?*

Inspired Insights

- The difference between "I can" and "I can't" is directly related to whether or not the goal is associated with something that ranks high on your values hierarchy.

- Living in alignment with your values allows you to tap into the natural confidence you have in the areas of greatest importance to you.

- There's no such thing as a human being with only low self-esteem. You simply have high self-esteem in areas associated with your highest values and low self-esteem in areas associated with your lowest values.

- Your greatest achievements may be in a form that you haven't recognized or acknowledged yet, but you are already successful in life.

- Knowing yourself and what is most important to you enables you to become crystal clear on your purpose and pursue an inspired destiny.

Words of Power

Choose at least one of the following affirmations and repeat it to yourself every day for at least the next month (ideally for the next few months). If this seems particularly challenging (or particularly rewarding), make a commitment to repeat it to yourself every day for the rest of your life.

I am a genius, and I apply my wisdom.

I am naturally confident in the areas that reflect my highest values.

I honor and acknowledge my unique form of success and achievement.

I am the master of my destiny.

PART II

LIFE SKILLS

CHAPTER 9

Discovering the Hero Within

"Nurture your mind with great thoughts.
To believe in the heroic makes heroes."
— **Benjamin Disraeli**

As you know, whenever you notice people supporting your higher values, you tend to elevate them in your mind. When you do so, these individuals begin to occupy space and time in your life, whether or not you've ever actually met them. They may become your heroes, and you might give them authority over your actions by attempting to live according to their values instead of your own.

As I've mentioned, whenever you align yourself with someone else's values, you begin to experience internal moral dilemmas and often need outside motivation to stay focused (because you're attempting to go against your own highest values). You may also hear yourself using more imperatives in your everyday speech, such as "I have to," "I need to," "I ought to," or "I should." Remember that when you inject someone else's values into your life, you become ungrateful for who you are. Feeling inferior and shrinking yourself leads you further away from your inspired destiny. In any area of your life that you don't feel empowered, someone else overpowers you.

Ralph Waldo Emerson wrote that "envy is ignorance [and] imitation is suicide." Indeed, when you're constantly trying to become more like others, you're killing a part of yourself . . . but that doesn't mean you can't resurrect your authentic self and begin to honor it.

I'm certain you've met people throughout your life whom you believed to be more spiritual, more intelligent, and more attractive than you; or perhaps you thought that they made better business decisions, amassed more wealth, experienced more fulfilling relationships, or even had more social connections. You likely compared yourself to these individuals and felt intimidated and much less successful. Remember that the moment you try to emulate somebody who has something you think you're missing, you minimize yourself. You give authority to him or her because that person's opinion becomes more valuable than your own. Without realizing it, you begin to hide your true identity and suppress your authentic self.

Have you ever been infatuated with someone and noticed that you slowed down or stopped doing what was important to you and started doing things just to please that particular person? You picked up a new set of values and tried to change yourself to be more like this "amazing" individual. But you can't be anyone but your authentic self. So what happens? Well, you split yourself, dividing awareness into the conscious and unconscious. Your conscious mind wants to be like the object of your affection, so you take actions to align with it. Meanwhile, your unconscious mind knows this isn't fulfilling your own true higher values and purpose, and resentment begins to build. You set goals that don't reflect your hierarchy of values, yet you also have trouble staying focused. You forget things often and wonder why you're so undisciplined.

This "self-sabotage" is actually the unconscious mind alerting you that your course has shifted away from your inspired purpose. You're off track and need to reexamine how your goals align with your values hierarchy. Whenever there's a conflict between your unconscious and conscious minds, your unconscious mind is going to win because it holds the key to your highest values. Remember that you're always focused, disciplined, and successful when you're consciously attuned to your authentic values.

When you admire qualities in others, it's the Universe's way to get you to wake up and recognize your own strengths—in other words, you need to realize that whatever you perceive in other people, you also have within yourself. You just haven't acknowledged it yet. The truth of who you are is far more spectacular than any imposed values from the outside. You are most powerful when you're honoring your authentic self by living in alignment with your highest values.

You are a wonderful person with something amazing to offer the world. Once you acknowledge your worth, then the world will acknowledge it in you. Treat yourself magnificently, and you'll be treated magnificently by the world. Unlock the incredible power of the hero within.

The Power of Your Hero

At one of my seminars in South Africa, there was a 17-year-old in attendance who was in the process of owning the traits of his inner hero. You see, I'd asked the participants to identify their heroes and make a list of their most admirable traits. Then they had to figure out where they already possessed those qualities and note the unique ways in which they expressed them in their own lives.

When the young man had completed the reflection process, I wanted to find out if he was getting the idea by asking, "Can you see that you aren't missing something—you just thought you were?"

He nodded and began to tear up a bit. This is what happens when you realize that you aren't missing anything at all. When you discover that, you become your whole self to the degree that you make everyone and everything yourself. Nothing is missing!

As I explained to the young man, "The purpose of having heroes isn't for you to idolize them. The real purpose is to see your reflection in them and their reflection in you. In other words, the qualities you admire in them already exist in you in the same degree. Can you see that the main point isn't to feel inferior or less than other people, no matter who they are?"

He said yes but was still very emotional. Curious to find out what he was thinking, I asked, "Who is your hero?"

"You, Dr. Demartini."

That took me aback. *"I'm your hero?"*

He nodded.

"Well, can you see that whatever you admire in me, you have in yourself?"

"Yes."

"What is your dream?"

"I'm going be an international professional speaker."

"So you know that a man with a mission like that has a message?"

"Absolutely."

I asked him to share his message in front of the group, and as he spoke, he delivered one of the most inspiring messages I'd ever heard. Everyone in the room, including me, was brought to tears and gave him a standing ovation.

The next day I was on a national radio show, and I told this story. The host was impressed, and as a result, the young man received several invitations to speak. My point is that as soon as he recognized that whatever greatness he saw in me, he possessed within himself, doors started opening. It was this recognition that put him on the path to realizing his own inspired destiny.

There are no limits to what you can do when you take the time to see that whatever you admire in others is also within you. If you go to the bank to borrow $100,000, the bank will ask you for $100,000 in collateral. If you don't have it, the bank won't give you the money. But as soon as you can demonstrate that you have it, you'll get the loan. Likewise, the world gives you what you acknowledge you already have. When you deny that you have it, you hold yourself back and limit your potential. You wouldn't be admiring your heroes if you didn't have within you what you perceive within them.

I've studied most of the philosophers, religious leaders, business magnates, and other celebrated people I respect—including Nobel Prize winners—and I've studied myself to find out where I have within me whatever I see in them. As I read their biographies, I underline every trait that I see and would love to discover within myself. This technique has had a profound effect on my life, and today I interact with many of the men and women I once admired from afar.

I am a busy teacher who is inspired by my profession, but I don't idolize anyone else in this industry. I don't minimize myself or wish that I could be more like another person; I simply appreciate and love my peers for who they are and for what they reflect in me. I'm willing to do whatever it takes to own all of the traits I've identified in them so that I can stand up onstage and share from my heart.

Whenever you're admiring other people, ask yourself where you have what you see in them. What form is it in? If you don't recognize your own unique expression of those traits, then you'll continue to submit to this outside authority. You'll assume that these folks have a better form of the trait than you do, and you'll begin to believe that something's missing within you.

Remember that your hierarchy of values dictates the form in which you express each trait. Where one person you admire has confidence in, say, business, you may have the same degree of confidence in your education. So you're not missing that trait! You may marvel at someone's dedication and focus in a certain sport, and when you look to see where you have this trait, you may find that you have incredible dedication and focus in your relationships. Owning the traits that you see in others within you will increase your gratitude and allow you to know with certainty that you have what it takes to live your inspired destiny.

Exercise: Get Inspired!

How Are You Like Your Hero?

1. Think of someone you admire. Who is your hero? This can be a person you've met or someone you've read about or seen on TV.

2. Write down his or her name and identify the trait you most admire.

3. Now jot down the initials of 20 to 50 people who see or have seen you express this trait. That is, think of when and where you've demonstrated this trait in your own unique way, and who saw you do it.

4. Continue adding initials until you can see with 100 percent certainty that you also have this trait within to the same degree.

Complete this exercise for your greatest heroes and role models, as well as anyone else you'd love to be like or associate with, and discover how you already possess all the revered traits you perceive in them. Read the life stories of all the famous people you look up to, and then find out where you have all of their traits and the ways in which you express them. Know that you're just as magnificent, powerful, influential, and dynamic as your greatest authorities so that you can discover your hero within.

Your Unique Form of Genius

Everyone's similar in their innermost soulful essence and different in their outermost existence. When you take time to find out how you express every single one of the traits you admire in someone else until you are 100 percent sure that you do have all of them, you wake up parts of yourself that have been hidden and reveal them to your conscious mind.

When this happens, your perception of who you are changes . . . and so does the world's perception of you. You express a unique form of genius in the areas of your highest values. You also have a vast supply of wealth and talent in the areas of your highest values. Unfortunately, many people diminish their own lives by believing that they're inferior to those whom they perceive are brighter, more successful, or more powerful . . . and then they wonder why they aren't inspired to get up in the morning and do what they love. Break free from this mind-set.

By my count, there are 4,600 character traits, and each one of us expresses all of them in similar or completely different ways. You express traits according to your unique hierarchy of values, and as you recognize and consciously own your many reflections of the world around you, you empower yourself. You're no longer blind, thinking that you're separate from (or somehow beneath) the people you admire, and you begin to value yourself.

Remember that when you value yourself, the world values you. When you appreciate yourself for who you are, the world appreciates you for who you are. When you love your own unique expression of every one of your traits, you give yourself the power to transform them into whatever you want them to be. By acknowledging the existence of what you perceive in others within yourself, the Universe helps you awaken the dormant powers you possess so that you can achieve your inspired purpose.

Inspired Insights

- Whatever you admire in other people, you also have within yourself.

- The purpose of your heroes is to wake you up so that you can recognize your own strengths and untapped potential.

- Every person is the same in essence and different in existence.

- There's incredible power in acknowledging that you possess every possible human character trait. When you express those traits according to your highest values, you are in perfect alignment with your inspired destiny.

Words of Power

Choose at least one of the following affirmations and repeat it to yourself every day for at least the next month (ideally for the next few months). If this seems particularly challenging (or particularly rewarding), make a commitment to repeat it to yourself every day for the rest of your life.

I acknowledge every human character trait within myself.

I love and appreciate myself, and the world loves and appreciates me.

*I have every single human character trait, and
I express traits according to my highest values.*

Every day I discover more and more of the hero within.

CHAPTER 10

Embracing the Duality of Life

"The mere fact that you have obstacles to overcome is in your favor."
— **Robert Collier**

Every situation has a positive side and a negative side. In truth, the Universe has a built-in duality—there is war and peace, kindness and cruelty, support and challenge, and so forth. Youth and age, poverty and wealth, joy and sorrow, solitude and multitude, illness and wellness, and failure and success arrive as pairs throughout life. It isn't possible to experience just one aspect, whether positive or negative.

Seeking a one-sided life is draining and disempowering, and it will hinder you from achieving your inspired dreams. The alternative? Learn to honor both aspects within every moment, and you'll create genuine, fulfilling love. Let me say it another way: *True love is a synthesis and synchronicity of complementary opposites.*

The Connection Between Your Emotions and Your Fulfillment

Whenever you perceive more pleasure than pain or more pain than pleasure, you experience lopsided emotions. (Let's define *emotion* as "energy set in motion.") Whether your emotions are positive or negative, this unbalanced mind-set keeps you distracted and thinking about the past or future instead of being centered in the present. Polarized emotions stop you from working toward your highest priorities, and you remain stuck on *XYZ* (your lowest values) instead of *ABC* (your highest values).

It's important to realize that you aren't here to run away from sadness to find happiness, avoid rejection and seek acceptance, or achieve success and never fail. Remember that both sides are integral to fulfillment, which is what you *are* here for.

For example, whenever you're not seeing the upside of an event or situation, you may feel resentful or fearful, and when you're not seeing the downside, you may feel infatuated or elated. In actuality, both aspects are simultaneously occurring—this is true in your individual, family, or social dynamics. Either side of any pair of polarities within the Universe is just "half-fillment" on its own. Genuine fulfillment is achievable only through acknowledging both sides of your existence at once.

My point is that if you don't take time to discover the hidden and synchronously balanced order that underlies your everyday apparent chaos, then you'll end up living in a world of stressful reactions. You react to whatever you're infatuated with or resentful of, whatever you admire or despise, and every thing or person you praise or reprimand. Whenever you seek a positive without a negative, pleasure without pain, or a support without a challenge, you set yourself up to experience the very thing you may be trying to avoid. It's wiser to be aware of the "pain," to know its presence, and to lessen its impact by acknowledging and appreciating its inherent gift. You dissolve imbalanced emotions when you train your mind to look for the other side of every event and realize that it's impossible to get anything other than a balanced whole.

Let's say that you've taken up running and really want to complete a marathon. You're infatuated with distance runners and are in awe of their endurance, lean bodies, and mental toughness. If you start training with only these positives in mind, though, you'll be quickly reminded of the other side of this sport once you take your first long run. Your body may ache and doubts may begin to set in, for example. You might even quit and wonder why anyone would ever want to do this!

But if you were to approach marathoning from a more balanced perspective (acknowledging from the outset that there will be days when you don't feel like training—when your feet hurt, your back's tight, and your mind tells you that it would make a lot more sense to spend the day on the couch), you could be ready to deal with these challenges or so-called negatives. When they inevitably occur, you would be able to simply observe what's happening and know that this is part of the package.

Your emotional misperceptions about the Universe can prevent you from understanding the innate balance that permeates your life no matter what you're doing. Anything you see as one-sided immediately becomes emotional baggage that you carry until it's resolved and freed. The more you're able to perceive both sides of every event, person, and place around you, the more you have access to your infinite potential to create the inspiring life you'd love. You experience the wisdom of the ages without the aging process and discover that there's nothing but love; all else is an illusion.

Seeing both aspects of the Universe liberates you by lightening your mind, thereby creating the experience of enlightenment. You'll transcend your old mind-set that keeps you stuck and repeating your revolving life patterns. Once your lopsided emotions are balanced, they become fuel for the journey ahead, helping you achieve your inspired destiny.

You will endure and even embrace both pain and pleasure equally when pursuing goals that are aligned with your highest values; on the other hand, you will try to avoid the pain and seek only pleasure in the areas of your lowest values. The former leads to the greatest accomplishments and fulfillment, while the latter leads to unrealistic expectations and often defeat.

Your Values and the Hidden Order of the Universe

You judge the events, people, and circumstances in your life according to your hierarchy of values. As I've mentioned, you label as "good" the things you perceive to support your higher values, and you label as "bad" the things that challenge your values. You'll notice that events in your life may at first seem terrible; and then days, weeks, months, or years later you come to realize that they had an equal dose of terrific in them. You'll also notice the reverse: some events that at first seem terrific prove to have had an equal measure of terrible when you gain the perspective of some days, weeks, months, or years. The bottom line is that the seemingly negative experiences always have hidden blessings, and the seemingly positive experiences always have hidden drawbacks.

It's wise to see beyond your perspective (which is filtered by your values) and discover the hidden order that permeates the Universe, every part of your life, and all of the events within it. The order is hidden because you haven't trained yourself to look for it or haven't taken the time to do so. You can become so busy with your daily routine and seeking what you believe is most missing in your life that you don't stop to really look at and listen to the ever-present field of intelligence that orchestrates and inwardly directs you.

Only being supported in your highest values results in your becoming more juvenile, dependent, and childlike; and only being challenged in your highest values stirs you to become more precocious, independent, and adultlike. Keep yourself accountable and continue looking for the balanced order in every moment and situation until you discover that you never get a one-sided experience of life. When you acknowledge this, you'll become more openhearted, empowered, and purposeful about fulfilling your unique inspired destiny.

You Grow Most on the Border of Support and Challenge

Research has shown that people achieve the most when they live on the border of "order" and "chaos," otherwise known as "support" and "challenge." You need people supporting you and being nice to you as well as people challenging you and being mean to you in order to maximize potential. If you don't have someone making you grow, then you automatically start to beat yourself up through your negative self-talk and thoughts. If you're avoiding obstacles (and seeking only what supports you, rather than what helps you grow), you'll keep attracting what you don't want until you learn to love and appreciate the service that such challenge provides you on the path to becoming who you'd love to be.

The people who support you, are nice to you, and try to please you actually foster more dependence and childishness in you. The people who challenge you, who are even mean to you and unconcerned about your pleasure, are the ones who genuinely contribute to your independence and maturity. If you experienced only support without challenge, you'd be totally unprepared for the world and vulnerable to being knocked out flat. If you experienced only challenge in your life, you might not have survived your childhood. You require both to maintain the equilibrium point called *love*.

The difference between entrepreneurs and intrapreneurs is that entrepreneurs perceived themselves more challenged early on in their lives, which fueled them to achieve great things and become the boss of others. Intrapreneurs (that is, those who prefer to be employed, without the risk or accountability of entrepreneurs), on the other hand, perceived that they got everything they wanted when they wanted it, and they became more dependent on that support. These individuals go out in the world looking for the same support from their childhood, seeking more pleasure over pain and support and security over challenge, and they often end up working for entrepreneurs.

In the moment you wisely embrace and acknowledge that you were equally supported and challenged in your life and realize that you were simultaneously praised and reprimanded, you come to discover what it truly means to be loved. The world around you has been assisting and guiding you to achieve what you're ultimately here for so that you may fulfill your inspired destiny, and it will continue to do so. Whatever experiences you've had throughout your life serve as "feedback loops" to get you to become clearer on what you'd love to dedicate your life to doing, being, and having.

Because your view of the world is filtered through your values hierarchy, you're constantly searching for whatever supports your beliefs and builds you up, but the Universe in its wisdom brings you people who challenge you *and* bring you down to keep your integral equilibrium. Remember that you're destined to experience both pain and pleasure; awareness of this keeps you balanced and poised in gratitude and appreciation for yourself, your life, and those around you. If you were to only receive praise from others, then you'd become overly elated about yourself. And if you were to only receive criticism, then you'd feel depressed, beat yourself up, and label yourself.

Equally embracing both aspects empowers you to transcend the positive and negative emotions and labels about your life and begin to act on high-priority tasks from inspiration. It doesn't mean that you never feel anything else, but in this empowered state, you also experience certainty, presence of mind, and gratitude. To the degree that you can acknowledge both sides of love (not only in the Universe but also within yourself), you awaken the true inspired you, who is extraordinary.

You Are a Two-Sided Being

You—like everything and everyone else—have two sides. You feel good about whatever you perceive to be more positive than negative about yourself: you build yourself up and can feel proud, cocky, puffed up, inflated, and focused on this part. You also feel bad about whatever you perceive to be more negative than positive in yourself: you tear yourself down and can feel depressed, ashamed, and unworthy. Since you're with yourself 24/7, expressing one side or the other nearly all the time, nobody raises you up or puts you down as much as you do. In order to fully embrace who you really are, you must acknowledge both sides of yourself . . . the so-called good and bad and positive and negative—the authentic, balanced you.

Most people accept without question the idea that you're supposed to be one or the other—that is, you're supposed to be nice and never mean, kind and never cruel, sweet and never bitter, and positive and never negative. This illusion distracts you from your purpose and why you're here. Carl Sagan observed that the Universe is far more magnificent than any fantasy or ideal that the human mind can impose upon it. Similarly, the human experience can be far more magnificent without the illusions that humans impose upon it. You require all parts of yourself to fulfill your mission! If one part wasn't necessary, it wouldn't exist. You're designed to express all aspects in order to love and appreciate who you are and to give others permission to do the same.

The challenges you face are there for equilibration; they are never mistakes. Often what you perceived as your greatest obstacles were exactly what you needed to find out who you are today and who you will be in the future. As a result, anything you can't be grateful for in your life becomes emotional baggage that gets carried with you—until you can find a way to balance and appreciate it. Remember that whatever you're grateful for becomes fuel for the journey because you can clearly see how it serves you in fulfilling your highest values, whether it was perceived as supportive or challenging.

From reading this book, you've probably realized that my childhood diagnosis of dyslexia has contributed greatly to who I am today. It led to my love of reading, and I've gone on to read tens of thousands of books and studied hundreds of intellectual disciplines. And one of the greatest conclusions I've drawn is that based on a scaled set of values (the hierarchy that's unique to each person), we all possess genius. We will exhibit "attention surplus order," or excessive attention, for what's most important to us, and attention deficit disorder, or what's known as ADD, for what's least important to us.

Some of us have a highly concentrated hierarchy of values, meaning that we narrowly focus on a few things we feel are vital, while others are more diversified. Oftentimes, when children have a highly concentrated set of values that deviates from their teachers' and parents', they're labeled as learning disabled, as I was, or as having ADHD (attention deficit/hyperactivity disorder). The truth is that these students still love to learn—everyone loves to learn—but *they love to learn what's most important to them.* They might have difficulty focusing on their studies or classes because those things aren't inspiring and don't directly relate to their values, but when you give these kids an activity they value, look out! They can sit there completely focused for hours and excel.

This applies to everyone: We all have an abundant attention span for what we value and a deficient attention span for what's low in our values hierarchy. Even adults tend to be fidgety or easily distracted when they're forced to focus on something that is of low value to them.

The key to tapping into your genius and unlocking your potential in whatever you're uninspired by or unmotivated to do is to take what is most important and link all of your tasks to these highest values, as I've done so many times throughout this book. Master the art of communication, and find out how these things are serving your highest values and assisting you to reach your goals. Recognize that both aspects always exist within you: lazy and industrious, inattentive and laser focused, fidgety and calm, and so on. Amazing results can be achieved when you do so! You can and will become inspired once your "challenges" are linked to your highest values.

So instead of using labels to dismiss another person's abilities, it's wise to take the time to identify his or her hierarchy of values and go from there. When you care enough to discover what your highest values are, you open up possibilities for yourself. And when you care enough to discover what others' highest values are, you open up possibilities for *them.*

I've worked with many young adults and children who have been labeled as having ADD or ADHD; and I've found them all to be quite ingenious, focused, and inspired. Once I communicated inside their highly concentrated values, they opened up and discovered that they too loved to learn. Instead of labeling people, you would do well to find out where their attention surplus order resides and honor their genius and confidence in those areas. Some of the world's greatest leaders, lateral thinkers, and pioneers were once assumed to be learning disabled. When they consciously or unconsciously discovered their highest values and began to pursue what was significant to them, they learned, grew, and rose to the top of their chosen fields.

This brings to mind a 13-year-old boy I once met, whose father drove four hours one evening so they could attend one of my talks. The father had brought a letter from the school principal stating that his son had certain learning disabilities, was hyperactive, and had even been expelled. I asked the boy what he loved to do and found out that he was really into cars. Throughout the rest of our conversation, the youngster would light up whenever we talked about his favorite subject. He told me that he wanted to work with cars when he grew up and didn't think his classes were going to help him achieve his dream.

I asked the father what would happen if the boy got a job at a dealership—possibly cleaning or any small task at first—just so he could be around and learn about cars. I predicted that his son would probably be a millionaire by 20 if he was allowed (and encouraged) to follow his dream.

Instead of putting someone in a box because of some diagnosis or label, it would be wiser to see all of the new possibilities that a unique life presents. I'm not saying that such diagnoses are useless; sometimes they help a person know what to do to counteract the perceived problem. What I want to be clear on is that these labels or boxes don't define anybody.

I knew a psychiatrist in Houston who had been given the label of ADHD for most of her life. She was a very active, multifaceted, brilliant, and highly driven individual who had extensive achievements, particularly within the hospital she managed. Although she talked quickly and acted hyper, she also had an electrified mind, filled with creative ideas that she implemented successfully. Once she found her niche, she excelled. Once *you* find what is most important to you, it becomes easier to put your energy in your highest values and pursue your inspired destiny.

Use what you've learned in this book to identify your highest priorities and then focus on those. Honor your authentic highest values, and don't submit to people on the outside who try to project their beliefs onto you. As your values evolve and you stay true to yourself, you're more and more likely to do something incredible with your life and make an amazing impact in the world. Focus on where you excel and what you love doing. Where are you concentrating your energy? Instead of trying to "fix" yourself or change to be like someone else, acknowledge your uniqueness and uncover your inner genius. Remember that every person possesses much wisdom in the form of his or her highest values.

If you're a teenager or a young adult and feel overwhelmed by people who may be scolding you, labeling you, or trying to change you, just know that this doesn't mean there's something wrong with you that has to be changed. You simply have a different form of genius and magnificence, a set of inner strengths that you may not have discovered. (Often what you're most inspired by isn't tested in schools.)

We all have responsibilities that we may not feel enthusiastic about, be it at school, work, or home. Link these responsibilities to what does inspire you by asking how doing these things or studying these topics is going to assist you to fulfill what is truly important to you. Keep asking and answering that question until you're just as inspired about doing these things and you can see how they're helping you feel fulfilled. When you do so, you'll be fueled up and ready to excel.

All of the challenges you face in life are designed to wake you up to the balance of love from within your being and from around the Universe. They're designed to help you see that you *do* have both sides of any human character trait and that you're worthy of love. This loving essence is essential for you to discover your purpose, live a meaningful life, and fulfill your inspired destiny.

You Never Miss Out on the Balance of Love

Whenever you beat yourself up, you'll notice something if you look closely: that you have simultaneously *built* yourself up somewhere else, but usually in another area of your life that ranks higher on your hierarchy of values. As other people perceive more of your self-deprecating side, they'll commonly try to lift or build your minimized self back up. Those who perceive you building yourself up will often try to bring your exaggerated self back down. When you feel humbled and pulled down by events, the people around you may try to lift you back up. If you walk along with your head down, looking like you've been left out in the rain, someone will probably try to cheer you up.

What would happen if you responded to praise by saying, "It's about time you noticed how great I am. You're so slow in learning that I'm amazing. Thank goodness you finally figured it out!" If you put yourself higher than where others imagined you in that moment, they'd attempt to bring you back down with a criticism or judgment, putting you "in your place." Anytime you reach beyond who you really are, you automatically attract things that bring you back down into equilibrium. You are here to be authentic—not elated or depressed, proud or ashamed.

Professional coaches work to make sure their clients don't get cocky just for that reason. For example, "caddie psychologists" will accompany golfers during a game to ensure that they don't get too high or too low emotionally. If they become overly elated or depressed about hitting a good or bad shot, their emotions can throw off their skills. This moderated volatility is crucial in determining the outcome of competitions or tournaments.

Whether you exaggerate or minimize the image of who you authentically are, you'll automatically attract correcting "factors" to neutralize you and bring you back into balance. Every time you experience a tragedy, for instance, you attract some comedy to lighten you up. Every time you're challenged, you attract support. Instead of getting humbling circumstances when you feel low, you attract pride-building circumstances, and instead of attracting low-priority distractions, you attract high-priority actions.

The very purpose of your relationships is to keep you grounded when you get overconfident and lift you up when you're down. Your friends, family, partner, teachers, and co-workers all play their part in keeping you balanced and experiencing true love. They bring harmony to the exaggerated or minimized you. Your most powerful self emerges in the moments when you're centered and inspired. When you're authentic, you radiate. You become original and creative, and you're inspired to do what you love and serve others.

The Great Discovery

Whenever someone praises you, someone else (somewhere) reprimands you at the exact same moment to balance you and keep you centered in love. If you look carefully, you'll see that every time you're challenged, you're also supported. There's never praise without criticism or criticism without praise. For every opportunity, there's a simultaneous obstacle. For every reward, there is a punishment; for every crisis, a blessing. There's never a door opening without one closing, and there's never a window closing without another one opening in the same moment.

Having demonstrated this balancing principle to thousands of people worldwide, I'm certain that regardless of age, race, color, creed, nationality, language, religion, culture, or tradition, we are all simultaneously embraced by a complementary dualism of love. We need both sides of love, both challenge and support, to keep us focused on the course to fulfilling our inspired destiny.

When you understand this principle—and begin to see it occurring all around you and across all seven areas of your life— you'll be able to tap into profound wisdom and a powerful understanding. (I refer to this process as The Great Discovery™.)

At one of my seminar events called The Breakthrough Experience® (where I teach the method you're about to undertake), I met a lady who had been born with vitiligo, a condition in which the skin loses melanin and looks blotchy and multicolored. This woman was light pink, dark brown, and white all mixed together; she looked something like a human patchwork quilt. Not only was her skin different, but she also had a memorable face with tiny ears and a nose that made her look a bit like a duck. Growing up, she'd felt ostracized as the other kids in school wouldn't go near her and called her the ugly duckling. This lady was lovely on the inside but had grown up feeling isolated, introverted, and ugly.

When I introduced her to The Great Discovery, she quickly uncovered the balance and order in the perceived criticisms—that is, she could finally acknowledge all the praise she'd received during her life despite the taunts from her peers. She realized that because she'd felt ugly as a child, she had always surrounded herself with beauty, which she was also acknowledged for. Today, she's one of the leading interior designers in the United States, and she fills her life, and others' lives, with amazing beauty.

A magnificent moment occurred at the seminar for this woman who'd spent her childhood believing she was only mocked, ridiculed, and isolated. One by one, she went to each of the people in the room (other members of the audience had stood up and played the role of her childhood tormentors) and *thanked* them from her heart. She'd gained an inspired vision and purpose to continue fostering her creativity and enabling others to see the beauty around them. When she realized what a blessing she'd received, she didn't question the price. If you feel that you've paid a high price at some time in your own life, find the simultaneous blessing and return to your center.

Saint Augustine taught that the will of God is equilibrium. The will of the Universe is for you to experience both sides of love in every moment.

Exercise: Get Inspired!

Experience The Great Discovery

1. Think of a moment in your life when you were strongly criticized or put down by someone. Write down what happened, where you were, when it occurred, and who criticized you. (For example, you could write: "Right before a break in class last week, my teacher . . .")

2. In your mind, revisit that specific moment, and answer the following questions: Who was lifting you up and looking up to you? Who was putting you on a pedestal when you were being criticized? (For example, "When my teacher was yelling at me, I looked over at my best friend who . . .")

The person who was supporting you in the exact moment when you were being criticized could be male or female, close or distant (such as a friend outside the room sending you a text message praising or thanking you), or even more than one person. Remember that the Universe doesn't present you with one side without also simultaneously presenting the other. Opposites are always simultaneous. You won't be able to perceive one without having the ability to perceive the other, for each perception comes with contrasts. Completing The Great Discovery process will help you realize that every event is equilibrating, and the truth is that there is nothing but this balance of love.

When you acknowledge that you experience both sides of life equally, when you enter the heart of love, you see that a magnificent hidden order orchestrates life. You can then stop living in one of the greatest illusions—that you can have pleasure without pain, praise without reprimand, nice without mean, or support without challenge. You can stop looking for a one-sided event in a two-sided Universe, which always proves frustrating, as it's impossible to ever receive anything but an equilibrating event. Emotions, like fear and guilt, will start to dissolve as you understand and experience the truth. When you embrace the balance, you'll realize that you will always be surrounded by love.

Inspired Insights

- True fulfillment comes when you acknowledge the duality of the Universe and stop seeking a one-sided experience of life.

- The emotions you experience are one-sided perceptions about events that have occurred in the past or might occur in the future.

- You grow maximally at the border of support and challenge. You need both to keep you focused and on the path to achieving your dreams.

- You're not only praised or reprimanded—know that you are loved at all times.

- You're not here for your life to get "easier." You're here to tackle your challenges and grow as you assume accountability in fulfilling your inspired destiny.

Words of Power

Choose at least one of the following affirmations and repeat it to yourself every day for at least the next month (ideally for the next few months). If this seems particularly challenging (or particularly rewarding), make a commitment to repeat it to yourself every day for the rest of your life.

I embrace the duality of life in the pursuit of my purpose.

*Whether I feel happy or sad, I am grateful
because it serves my mission.*

I am most powerful when I embrace my supports and my challenges.

Love is a balance of opposites, so everything is an expression of love.

CHAPTER 11

Conquering Your Biggest Life Challenge

"A crisis is an opportunity riding the dangerous wind."
— **Chinese proverb**

Earlier in this book, I shared with you what my first-grade teacher told me: that I would never be able to read or write and that I wouldn't go far in life. And you know what? I *believed* that for ten years . . . until the time when I almost died in Hawaii after consuming toxic seeds. That led me to Paul Bragg and from that moment, I've been inspired to pursue what I'm doing today. I didn't know how I was going to achieve my dreams; I just visualized myself doing it and got into action.

As I've mentioned, when my parents encouraged me to take the GED exam, I guessed my way through it while silently repeating the affirmation: *I am a genius, and I apply my wisdom.* When I found out that I'd passed, my mom persuaded me to take the college entrance exam. Using my patented method of guessing and affirming, I passed once again. After that, I started to really believe that I *was* a genius, and I *was* applying my wisdom! I grew even more confident when I realized that all of the kids I went to junior high with had actually finished high school and applied for college a month after I did. This meant that I was actually *ahead* of my class now, even though I'd spent four years surfing in Texas, California, Mexico, and on the North Shore of Oahu.

I also briefly mentioned that when I started taking college courses, my learning difficulties resurfaced, and I began to struggle. I'd like to share a particular story in more detail because it was another significant turning point in my life. I hit rock bottom when I took a test and got a 27 when I needed a 72 to pass the class. It seemed that I was still "dyslexic," and I somehow even managed to get a backward score. I was devastated.

Afterward, I sat in my car and broke down. I was no longer thinking about my powerful affirmation—instead, my first-grade teacher's discouraging words came rushing back. As I drove home (I actually had to pull over a few times because I was crying so hard), all I could hear in my mind was her voice.

When I got to my parents' house, I walked into the living room and collapsed. I curled up under the Bible stand and just lay there, having lost my vision and inspired purpose. I was still there when my mother came home from shopping and found me.

"John? What happened? What's wrong?"

"I blew it, Mom. I failed the test. I needed a 72 to pass, and I got a 27. I guess I never will amount to anything."

My mother just stood there and stared at me. Then she knelt down beside me, put her hand on my shoulder, and looked me straight in the eyes. And in that moment, she said something that changed my life.

"Son, if you become a great teacher and travel the world like you dream of, if you go back to Hawaii and surf every day, or even if you end up on the streets and panhandle for a living, I want you to know that your father and I are going to love you no matter what you do."

I broke down again, and my mother was in tears, too. My hand spontaneously clenched into a fist, and as I closed my eyes, I saw the same vision I'd experienced the night I met Paul Bragg:

me standing on a balcony speaking in front of a million people. I said to myself, *I'm going to master this thing called <u>reading,</u> and I'm going to master this thing called <u>studying.</u> Then I'm going to master <u>teaching, healing, philosophy,</u> and <u>speaking.</u> I'm going to do whatever it takes! I'm going to travel whatever distance and pay whatever price to achieve my dream, and I'm not going to let any human being (not even myself) stop me.* As my mind raced, I felt something indescribable: I reached a point where my inspired vision was stronger than any obstacle on Earth.

I hugged my mother and then locked myself in my room. I found a dictionary, opened it up to the first page, and started reading. Even if I didn't understand something, I kept on reading. I also made sure that I learned 30 new words a day, and every night my mom would quiz me. I continued studying to build my vocabulary so that I could read with greater confidence, understanding, and retention.

Today, having left those particular trials and triumphs far behind me, I'm absolutely certain that all of us have the strength and potential within to overcome our biggest challenges and do something truly amazing. It would be impossible to convince me otherwise.

When you're aligned with your highest values and know what you'd love to do with your life, nothing can stop your sheer determination and ability to rise above and conquer your biggest obstacles.

Your Greatest Challenges Create Your Greatest Achievements

It's interesting to note that many world-renowned scientists, athletes, and philosophers, and other famous men and women were either adopted or orphaned at a young age. Some of the world's richest people were actually born into extreme poverty. From the outside, these circumstances may appear to be overwhelming, yet this is where these individuals were able to foster that inner power to help them survive and even rise above their surroundings.

Whatever you perceive as your greatest challenge—whatever you think stops you from living your purpose—may be the very thing you need to achieve your inspired destiny. Breaking through your old beliefs will free you from the past and help you realize your dreams.

Exercise: Get Inspired!

Identify Your Biggest Challenges

1. Write down your biggest challenge. What has been the most difficult thing for you so far? (For example, "Growing up with only one parent has been a huge challenge for me.")

2. Take out your hierarchy of values, and write down your top three.

3. Now jot down 20 to 50 ways in which your biggest challenge has assisted you in helping to fulfill your highest values. (Based on the previous example, you might write: "I learned how to communicate with people. I became independent and didn't rely upon others to take care of me. I left home at an early age but learned how to support myself.")

Find Out How Your Life Challenges Shape Who You Are

— Write down your top-three values. (For example, "My top-three values are physical health, education, and my career.")

— Identify the challenges you experienced that created what is most important to you today. What difficulties have you faced? Where have you felt that you weren't expressing your top values? What do you feel is missing in your life? (For example, "I value good health because I was very ill as a child. Education is important to me because my siblings all did well in school, and I've always wanted to do as well as they did. When I was a teenager, I was unsure about my future, so I searched for a fulfilling career to fill up that uncertainty.")

Overcoming Your Biggest Challenge to Live Your Destiny

What appears to be your biggest challenge may actually be the very thing that you are destined to overcome. Any person, place, thing, idea, or event in your life that you aren't grateful for becomes baggage instead of fuel for the journey ahead. Whatever you perceived as your greatest challenge during your youth can often be the source of your dreams and aspirations. It is wise to be appreciative of these challenges, for they have the power to lead you to inspiring places.

Childhood illnesses and diseases can create the most influential healers or athletes, for instance. People who feel unworthy may foster a powerful drive within and make an outstanding contribution to the world in order to achieve self-worth and a sense of wholeness. And great poverty can be the catalyst for great wealth.

Remember that your values are formed from your challenges and often shape who you are today and who you will become. Learn to be grateful for whatever occurs by asking how these obstacles have served you. Your "setbacks" guide you into doing exactly what you love so that you'll achieve a meaningful life.

Inspired Insights

- The further down and out you've been, the further up and in you can go.

- Great challenges create great achievements. Many of the most successful people throughout history experienced adverse circumstances that drove them to achieve their dreams.

- What challenges you the most may be the very thing you're destined to overcome, and may even hold the key to living a meaningful, inspiring life.

Words of Power

Choose at least one of the following affirmations and repeat it to yourself every day for at least the next month (ideally for the next few months). If this seems particularly challenging (or particularly rewarding), make a commitment to repeat it to yourself every day for the rest of your life.

*I am wise, for I instantaneously recognize
that every crisis is a blessing.*

Every life challenge fuels me to ever-greater achievements.

The further down and out I have been, the further up and in I can go.

I let no challenge stop me from achieving my inspired destiny.

CHAPTER 12

How to Deal with . . .

"The future depends on what we do in the present."
— **Mahatma Gandhi**

In this chapter, I'll cover the nine most significant emotional challenges you may experience along the way to fulfilling your inspired destiny. Here, you'll pick up powerful life skills for effectively and efficiently overcoming or benefiting from each one of your challenges. You'll learn the truth behind fear, guilt, resentment, regret, and other emotions that might be running your life and seemingly stopping (or at least hindering) you from moving forward on the path to achieving your dreams.

Any lopsided emotions you have pull your mind into focusing on the past or the future. You get taken out of the present moment and your attention becomes scattered as you try to deal with your memories of what has already happened and your imaginings of what could happen and what might take place down the road. Whenever you take yourself out of the present and become emotionally distracted, you react to the world around you and allow your circumstances to run your life. In this state, you limit your power and potential to create the life you'd love.

There are several exercises in this chapter. As you read each section, be sure to complete each exercise and apply the principles to your everyday life. By doing so, you'll balance any misperception about what has occurred in the past and fears about what may happen in the future.

1. Future Fear

Like a lot of children, I was afraid to go in my room alone in the dark because I thought there was a bogeyman in there. My father told me, "I'll walk you to your room once and show you how to turn on the light, but from then on, you have to do it yourself."

During the day, I practiced running down the hall and flipping on the light as I leapt into my room. Then at night, I'd run and jump across the hallway, flick the light switch as I came flying into the room, and then stand there, poised to take on whatever might be waiting for me. I wore a Zorro outfit and carried a plastic sword, and I was ready to face my fears.

What do you know? The bogeyman never showed.

You may have to walk through your own darkened doorways and actively turn on the light to conquer whatever frightens you. Remember that fear is an illusion sparked by the idea that you can experience one side of something without simultaneously experiencing the other. The Universe maintains harmony at all times, so your fear will dissolve when you realize that it's impossible to ever receive more negative than positive. When you take a look at the moments where you thought you endured more pain than pleasure and see the truth of love, you'll realize that you have no evidence where you encountered one side without simultaneously encountering the other. It takes an honest probing to discover the ever-present, synchronous balance of love.

Exercise: Get Inspired!

Dissolve Any Fear

1. Consider what you're most afraid of happening in the future. (For example, you might write: "I'm afraid my friends will reject me.")

2. Now come up with 20 to 50 *benefits* that you'd experience if this were to happen. (For example, "I could be the trendsetter instead of a follower.")

3. Write down 20 to 50 drawbacks if the thing that you fear *doesn't* happen. (For example, "I'd still be the one who always fits in instead of standing out and possibly making a difference.")

4. Recall a specific moment in the past where your fear occurred. (For example, "I wore the wrong outfit to a party and felt totally rejected.")

5. In your mind, go into that specific memory.

6. Now jot down 20 to 50 *benefits* you got out of that experience. (For example, "I spent time doing what I really wanted to do instead of trying to be someone I wasn't.")

7. Write down 20 to 50 drawbacks if the event *hadn't* occurred. (For example, "I wouldn't know my values as clearly as I do today.")

Find out the ways in which actually experiencing what you're afraid of would *help* you in fulfilling your highest values. How would this event actually allow you to grow and become more of who you'd love to be?

2. Past Guilt

No matter what you have or haven't done, you're worthy of love. That's true for everyone, yet many of us allow our guilt to shade our perception of worthiness. Guilt, after all, is the assumption (not necessarily based on facts) that in the past, you caused more pain than pleasure, more loss than gain, more negativity than positivity, or more drawbacks than benefits to yourself or someone else. Anytime you feel bad about something you have or haven't done, you accumulate emotional baggage and hold yourself back from believing that you deserve what you would love.

Guilt can keep you bound in an altruistic state of being where you continue giving (money, time, energy, and so on) to compensate for past actions, whether they were real or imagined. You can wind up servicing an unpayable debt to the people you think you owe.

Remember that it isn't possible to do something that someone perceives as "painful" without him or her simultaneously experiencing an equal and opposite "pleasure." Positive and negative are always paired together. The human mind will maintain an outward or inward balance, even if it has to dissociate into delusional fantasies to obtain it. Dissolving your guilt clears out your one-sided perception of past events and allows you to see that you're worthy of love no matter what. You're most powerful when you're neither altruistic nor narcissistic, but balanced and integrated instead.

Exercise: Get Inspired!

Dissolve Any Guilt

1. Recall a time when you did (or didn't do) something that you think caused someone more pain than pleasure. What happened that you still feel guilty about? (For example, "I ran out on my brother when he needed me.")

2. Jot down what happened, as well as 20 to 50 ways in which what you did or didn't do *benefited* the other person. (For example, "My brother got the chance to bond with his girlfriend.")

3. Write down 20 to 50 ways in which it would have been a drawback to the person if you had done *the opposite* of what you did in the moment. (For example, "If I had stayed, my brother wouldn't have the strong relationship with his girlfriend that he does now.")

4. Think back on the moment when you think you caused the person more pain than pleasure, and identify who was doing the opposite for that person in the moment. (For example, "My other family members were there for my brother when I wasn't.")

3. Resentment

Much like guilt, resentment is the assumption that in the past you experienced more pain than pleasure, more loss than gain, more negativity than positivity, and more drawbacks than benefits from someone around you. Whenever you resent someone for something that you perceive they did or didn't do, you place the person in a pit and label his or her action (or inaction) as "bad."

The result is another form of emotional baggage that you'll carry until you balance your perspective and free yourself. Just as it is unwise to put anyone on a pedestal, it is also unwise to put someone in a pit—but everybody is worth putting in your heart.

Exercise: Get Inspired!

Dissolve Any Resentment

1. Choose a person you feel resentment toward. (For example, "My employer.")

2. Write down the person's name and the human character trait that you most resent or despise in him or her. (For example, "My manager Tom is critical of me.")

3. Look through your life to find where and when you've expressed this trait to one or many people to the same degree. Be sure to consider the present moment as well as the past. (Remember that you have every trait, and you never gain or lose a trait. You only change the form of its expression.)

4. Jot down the initials of people who have seen you expressing this trait. Continue recording initials until you recognize that you possess the trait 100 percent as much as you perceive the person you've resented does. Remember to look in the past as well as the present to find where you express this trait.

5. Write down 20 to 50 ways in which this person has helped or served you by expressing this trait. (For example, "This gave me an opportunity to pinpoint my weaknesses and refine my skills.")

6. Note where or when the person exhibits the opposite trait of the one you dislike. (For example, "Tom praised me when I got us a new client.")

7. At the exact moment where the person expressed the trait you disliked, who was expressing the opposite trait to you?

8. Write down 20 to 50 drawbacks if the person you feel resentment toward had expressed the opposite trait in the moment. (For example, "If my manager hadn't criticized me, I wouldn't have improved my skills and gotten a promotion.")

4. Regret

Again, this lopsided emotion is a perception that you did or didn't do something that caused you or another person more pain than pleasure, more negativity than positivity, more loss than gain, or more drawbacks than benefits. Regret is an assumption that if you had done the opposite, your life or someone else's would have in some way been better than what it was in that moment. This mind-set prevents you from making clear decisions because you fear that you'll repeat your so-called mistakes.

Exercise: Get Inspired!

Dissolve Any Regret

1. Write down an action that you regret. (For example, "I shouldn't have changed the topic that I was studying in class.")

2. Write down 20 to 50 *benefits* of that action. (For example, "By changing topics, I got to learn something that really assisted me in my job and was even able to share the information with my co-workers.")

3.   Write down 20 to 50 drawbacks that would have occurred if you hadn't done the regretted action. (For example, "I was feeling bored and uninspired. I probably would have lost enthusiasm for my career altogether.")

5. Sadness/Circumstantial Depression

Whenever you have a fantasy about how you think your life should be instead of being grateful for how it is, you split yourself in two. The fantasy appears to be more positive than negative, and as a result you compare your reality to it. You then become sad and depressed whenever you perceive that your life doesn't match the unrealistic ideal in your mind.

When you dissolve those unhealthy fantasies, your sadness or depression simultaneously dissolves. You become appreciative of your life the way it is and let go of any unrealistic expectations.

Exercise: Get Inspired!

Dissolve Any Sadness/Circumstantial Depression

1.   Recall a time when you felt sad or depressed, and write down the event that triggered it. (For example, "I started feeling down three weeks ago when my partner left me.")

2.   Ask yourself what ideal you were holding on to at the time. Your fantasy is what you perceive would have been better in your life if things had happened differently in that moment. (For example, "We were supposed to get married and have a happy life together.")

3.   Pretend for a moment that things had happened as you thought they should have, and write down the drawbacks you would have experienced if this imagined fantasy

had come true. (For example, "If we were still together, I wouldn't spend as much time with my friends as I do now. I realize now that I was always trying to please my partner and felt insecure about our relationship.")

6. Intimidation

Eleanor Roosevelt once remarked, "No one can make you feel inferior without your consent." In other words, intimidation is more about how you perceive others in comparison to yourself than how others act toward you. To stop minimizing yourself and feeling inferior (instead of feeling grateful for what you have and the ways in which people bring out all of the traits in you), appreciate yourself more and honor your uniqueness.

If you feel intimidated by people, it's likely that you've placed them on a pedestal. It's wise to take them down from that pedestal, and identify the admired traits that you perceive in those individuals. Then see where *you* possess those qualities to the same degree. Remember that others will control your life when you have an imbalanced perspective, but you control it when you maintain a balanced, loving viewpoint.

Exercise: Get Inspired!

Dissolve Any Intimidation

1. Think about a person who intimidates you. Whom do you feel less than, dominated by, or controlled by?

2. Write down the individual's name and two specific human character traits you believe this person has that contribute to your feelings of inferiority. (For example, "Cathy is outspoken and highly intelligent.")

3. For each trait, write down the initials of 20 to 50 people in your life who see or have seen this trait in you until you own it 100 percent.

4. Write down the ways in which you benefit from this person having these two traits—in other words, how they *serve* you. (For example, "Cathy's outspokenness encourages me to empower myself and stand up for my beliefs. Cathy's intelligence challenges me to study, increase my vocabulary, and ask more questions.")

7. Stress

In my experience, the more stress you feel, the less able you are to adapt to a fluctuating environment. Whenever you expect parts of your life to stay the same and then they suddenly change, you're likely to feel overwhelmed—unless you're prepared to adapt and adjust as needed. Anytime you feel pressured or anxious, your mind and body also work overtime.

You might experience stress when you're planning to move to a new city or state, settling into a new job, speaking in front of a large audience, or studying for an exam. No matter what you're doing, feeling overly tense or pressured by events or other people won't necessarily help you achieve your goals.

Exercise: Get Inspired!

Dissolve Any Stress

1. Identify an event in your past, present, or future that you feel or have felt stressed about. (For example, "I'm stressed about taking my final exams.")

2. Write it next to the top-two entries in your hierarchy of values.

3. Write down 20 to 50 ways in which this stressful event *serves* or *benefits* you and helps you fulfill your two highest values. (For example, if your top values are "social" and "family," you may say, "I get to ask my family to support me while I'm studying. I'm learning to manage my time wisely so that I can study as well as spend time with my friends. Because my time is limited, I value every moment I spend with my loved ones even more.")

4. Write down 20 to 50 drawbacks that would arise if this event didn't occur. (For example, "I wouldn't get to bond with my closest friends. I wouldn't appreciate my parents' knowledge when they help me study. I wouldn't feel that I work hard and earn my results.")

8. Grief and Loss

Many people live with the perceptual illusions of gain and loss, while true masters simply exist in a world of transformation. What these wise individuals understand is that nothing is ever gained or lost—rather, they know that everything changes. This includes people, relationships, money . . . you name it. You don't gain or lose anything through death, breakups, bankruptcy, or the like—when things change, they simply take on new forms.

Whenever you perceive that a state of being (such as "life" and "death") or a character trait (such as "close" or "distant") has more good than bad, more benefits than drawbacks, more positives than negatives, or more pleasure than pain, you set yourself up for feelings of grief in the moment when you perceive its loss. You also set yourself up for feelings of elation and emotional high whenever you perceive its gain. Remember, these emotions are due to imbalanced perceptual illusions.

The beauty of any "loss" is that it creates room for something new. If everything in your life was permanent, you'd become bored by the same routine. Be grateful for the transformation that occurs in all areas of life in every moment of every day.

Exercise: Get Inspired!

Dissolve Any Grief and Loss

1. Write down the name of someone you miss or perceive you've lost.

2. What do you most miss about this person? Write down his or her specific human character trait that you perceive you lost. (For example, "I really miss my sister's sense of humor.")

3. Write down 20 to 50 people and situations where this trait has surfaced elsewhere in your life. (For example, "My father started cracking jokes when my sister left. Some of my friends took me to a comedy festival last month.")

4. Write down 20 to 50 *benefits* of the new form(s). (For example, "I get to hang out with more than one person and have greater variety in my social life. I got to bond with my father.")

5. Write down 20 to 50 drawbacks of the old form. (For example, "Sometimes I was the target of my sister's humor. My sister demanded my full attention, and I had to consider her needs much of the time.")

9. Betrayal

Betrayal is a bit more complicated and requires more explanation than the other emotional challenges. This is because it's necessary to discard your previous beliefs about this concept and open up to a whole new meaning. In essence, *no one ever betrays you.*

When you feel betrayed, it's because you've had unrealistic expectations that people will live outside their values and within yours. In other words, you projected your values onto others, and when they behaved according to their own hierarchy of values, you felt hurt. Betrayal springs out of self-righteousness: *My values are the right ones, so others ought to behave according to them.* Even if you're "generous" enough to admit that different value hierarchies are valid, you may be clinging to the idea that at least one of your values is somehow better than someone else's, or that everyone should live by your rules in a certain area of life. This, however, automatically increases the probability of your feeling betrayed. In addition, whenever you're "self-wrongeous" (minimizing yourself by trying to live according to someone else's values), you'll feel as if you're betraying yourself because you aren't being true to your own authentic values.

Yet, as you now know, everyone naturally lives according to his or her own values, no matter what. Consider this example: Let's say that one of your friends asks if you'd like to go shopping next Tuesday. It sounds fun, and since you have nothing else scheduled for the day, you accept. Then out of the blue, the guy you've been interested in for the past six months asks you to go to a concert with him on the same day. When he inquires if you're available, you say, "Of course!"

But remember that you already made plans with your girlfriend. Now you're going to ditch her because, at any one moment in your life, you're going to make decisions that fulfill your highest values most. If going out with this guy is higher on your values list than going shopping, then you'll figure out how to politely dump your friend.

Just to make it interesting, let's say that your friend is also interested in dating this guy. Now you're planning to go out with the person she's been fantasizing about, *and* you're going to cancel plans with her so that you can spend time with him. Let's also say that the reason she wanted to go shopping was to buy a new outfit to get this guy's attention. When you explain the situation to her, you're going to have to be very thoughtful and caring. Otherwise, she probably isn't going to be inclined to talk to you, since she'll be feeling like you've betrayed her.

The truth? You just challenged and supported her values.

Let's not stop there, though. You just got another offer for the same day. Let's say you were invited to fly on a private jet to Italy with your favorite rock group (and its smoking-hot lead singer). What would you do then? Not only have you broken plans with your friend, but you're now going to cancel your date, telling him that something else came up so that you can jet off to Europe.

The underlying motivation? Something even more significant that met your values came up so you dumped the other two. All of your decisions were made according to what you thought would give you the most advantages over disadvantages and most rewards over risks. When something came into your life that was more meaningful, powerful, or valuable to you, you changed your plans to do it. You're always going to focus upon what gives you the greatest fulfillment in your hierarchy of values.

Realize that nobody betrays you. You may, however, betray yourself by putting false expectations on other people to live outside their higher values. When you expect friends, family members, or co-workers to do something that's high on your values list and low on theirs, they probably won't be reliable. For instance, if your sibling's highest values are her children and you have an expectation that she'll get a job that requires a commitment to working overtime, you're setting yourself up to feel betrayed. If you're expecting your partner to help you pick out an outfit at the mall but you know that he or she can't stand shopping, chances are that your plans will keep being delayed, and you've set yourself up for feeling betrayed.

The only thing you can legitimately expect people to do is live within their hierarchy of values. The reality is that others aren't committed to you; they're committed to their values and to fulfilling what's important to them. But you aren't committed to anyone else either; you're committed to fulfilling your own highest values.

Exercise: Get Inspired!

Dissolve Any Betrayals

1. Recall a specific moment in your life when you felt betrayed. Think about the highest values of the "betrayer," and compare it to your own values hierarchy. In what ways were you projecting your values onto the other person? Were your expectations unrealistic?

2. When has someone accused you of betrayal? Write down the details of what took place. Examine your hierarchy of values and compare it to what you were supposed to do or say (that is, whatever the "betrayal" was). Do you see the ways in which the "accuser" was projecting his or her higher values onto you rather than appreciating that you were simply being true to your own? Were this person's expectations unrealistic?

Freeing Yourself to Live Your Inspired Destiny

Whenever you perceive more positives than negatives (infatuation) or more negatives than positives (resentment) in any person or event in your life, you'll become focused on fantasies of the future or memories of the past while missing out on the present. Remember that balancing your emotions clears your mind and reveals your ever-present inspired destiny. Set yourself free from your one-sided perceptions about yourself, other people, and the world you live in!

Inspired Insights

- Anytime you're focused on emotions about the past or the future, you distract yourself from the power of the present moment.

- When you let go of the past and dissolve any fear about the future, you become inspired and grateful for your life the way it is in the here-and-now.

- Lopsided emotions—if sustained and not understood— can hinder you from your potential, which is living a magnificent life and fulfilling your inspired destiny.

Words of Power

Choose at least one of the following affirmations and repeat it to yourself every day for at least the next month (ideally for the next few months). If this seems particularly challenging (or particularly rewarding), make a commitment to repeat it to yourself every day for the rest of your life.

*I set myself free from illusions of the past and the future
and become powerfully focused in the here-and-now.*

*I attune my thoughts and focus upon taking
high-priority actions toward fulfilling my dreams.*

*I have realistic expectations of myself and others
to live according to our unique sets of values.*

*I know that all people are committed to
fulfilling their own hierarchy of values.*

CHAPTER 13

Changing Your Values

"Tell me what you value, and I'll tell you where you're headed."
— **Anonymous**

You now know that your hierarchy of values dictates your destiny; and your values determine how you perceive the world, what actions you take (or don't take), and what you ultimately achieve in your life.

You also know that when you set goals that are strongly aligned with your authentic highest values, you become inspired, empowered, and dedicated to your purpose. And when you set goals that aren't aligned with your highest values, you procrastinate, frustrate, and hesitate, requiring outside motivation to get you to do something that doesn't inspire you. You're more likely to set achievable goals in reasonable time frames when your goals are directly linked to your desired outcome. Unless you genuinely value something, you won't be willing to persevere.

This boils down to two options: Either create goals that you're sure are aligned with your highest values (what your life demonstrates is most important to you), *or* change your values so that they're aligned with your goals. Didn't think you could do that? Well, you can! It is absolutely possible to rearrange your hierarchy and link new values to your goals so that they line up with your objective. Let's start with an exploration of how you can tell when this might be wise to do.

Recognize Your Self-Defeating Patterns

Of course you're aware that if your goals and values aren't aligned, the chances of achieving your inspired purpose seem to decrease. Pay attention to your everyday progress, as this will offer you clues to whether or not you have harmony in this area. When you're congruent and on track, your life will demonstrate that you're indeed moving closer to your desired outcome because you're focused on what's most important to you. Whenever you realize that you're not naturally taking steps toward your goals, this means that your goals are not those that are truly the most important to you, and they are incongruent.

The truth is that you've been attempting to work toward something that doesn't reflect your highest values. This is how you create seemingly self-defeating cycles of giving up on tasks or struggling through them. These patterns are simply signs indicating what you already know deep down: your goals don't align with your highest values.

Let's say, for example, that you wish to increase your income. If spending time with your family ranks higher than working, you're likely to struggle to find the time and energy in order to make extra money. Unless your financial area of life is also very high on your values list, you'll be more likely to procrastinate, hesitate, and feel frustrated.

Perhaps your goal is to exercise regularly so that you can lose weight, but education ranks higher on your hierarchy. Unless you can clearly see how working out helps you get where you'd love to be academically, then you'll probably need a lot of outside incentives to maintain a consistent exercise routine. Your highest value makes you want to spend your time reading, researching, and studying to master your subjects and achieve high grades.

When you set goals from an inspired mind-set (where you're in touch with your authentic self and in harmony with your highest values), you'll naturally have a much higher probability of achieving those goals. You'll become dedicated and focused on your desired outcome. Extraordinary individuals make a difference in the world and change the course of history through creating and enhancing goals that complement what is most crucial to them.

Remember that whenever your life is showing you that your goals aren't aligned with what is most important to you, you do have the power to change your values to match those goals.

Exercise: Get Inspired!

Change Your Hierarchy of Values to Align with Your Goals

1. Select a value you wish to place higher up in your hierarchy. (For example, "Wealth.")

2. Write it alongside your current top-three values. (For example, "My top-three values are relationships, socializing, and beauty/attractiveness.")

3. Now write down 100 to 500 ways in which the value you want to move up assists you in fulfilling your current highest values. (For example, ask yourself how having more money would help you better fulfill your relationships, your ability to socialize, and your physical beauty. You might write: "If I make more money, I can start saving up to provide a secure future with my partner. I can afford to use a portion to go out regularly and do things with my friends. I can visit my salon more often, which helps me feel more attractive.")

4. Now write down 100 to 500 ways in which *not* honoring the value is a drawback to your current highest values. (For example, "Sometimes I have to stay at home because I'm short on cash, so I miss out on fun events with my friends. My outfits don't really flatter my figure, but I can't afford to buy new clothes.")

To powerfully shift your hierarchy of values, be sure to write down no fewer than 100 benefits and drawbacks for the above exercise. When you've created the new "void" and elevated a value, you'll automatically start to empower that area of life and take action toward achieving the new outcome. Ensuring that your goals and values are aligned is an essential part of being able to do what you love and love what you do. This is one of the keys to living your inspired destiny.

Inspired Insights

- You have two choices when you set your goals: come up with goals that are aligned with your highest values, or change your values so that they reflect your goals.

- So-called self-defeating patterns are feedback and signs that you're setting goals that aren't in harmony with what is most important to you.

- When your goals and values are parallel, you become inspired, empowered, and dedicated to living your purpose.

- You can raise or lower values in your hierarchy to empower different areas of your life.

Words of Power

Choose at least one of the following affirmations and repeat it to yourself every day for at least the next month (ideally for the next few months). If this seems particularly challenging (or particularly rewarding), make a commitment to repeat it to yourself every day for the rest of your life.

My hierarchy of values dictates my inspired destiny.

I am wise, for I make sure that my goals are attuned with my highest values.

My goals help me amplify and manifest my greatest dreams.

I am in touch with my authentic self and focused on my purpose.

CHAPTER 14

Do What You Love, Love What You Do

"Each man has his own vocation. The talent is the call.
There is one direction in which all space is open to him."
— **Ralph Waldo Emerson**

While on the path to achieving your dream career, there may be times where you're working at a job or taking on a responsibility that seems lower on your values list. If you aren't able to pinpoint how your current duties are assisting you in fulfilling your highest values, it would be wise to find out how they do as soon as possible. In what ways are those daily tasks helping you get where you'd love to be? Discovering this allows you to become present and energized, as well as grateful for the opportunity you have to serve others right now.

When you're lackadaisical about your work, you repeatedly experience the Monday-morning blues. Every Wednesday becomes "hump day," and by the end of the week, you practically shout "TGIF!" throughout the office. You can almost guarantee that you'll procrastinate, hesitate, feel frustrated, and be easily distracted in your lifeless daily activities. Other things will come up, and you'll create a variety of excuses to get out of doing what isn't fulfilling. You'll go through life waiting to get out of or away from your job instead of being psyched to go to work each day.

When you hear the common advice to "do what you love, and the money will follow," this doesn't mean that there's only one possible path for you, or that your work will finally be fulfilling and life will be grand the moment you finally find your ideal profession. The wise person understands that the key is to love what you do, *no matter what you do*. Either go and do what you love, or love what you do. It's all about your perception. If you had the skill and drive to land the job, then you have the skill and drive to love it.

When you're able to see how your current role helps you achieve your goals, you'll feel energized and jump out of bed in the morning in order to do what you love. As you realize how your role fulfills your highest values, you'll tap into your inner wisdom and become more innovative and creative. When you're inspired—by definition, you have the "spirit within"—you feel enthusiastic. In such a state, you are the master of your destiny, taking charge of your magnificent life.

Being Self-Determined

Many employers don't make hiring decisions based on potential employees' values, and they usually don't take the time to communicate job descriptions in relation to an applicant's highest values. In the early 1960s, the motivational theorist Douglas McGregor asserted that there are two ways to manage people: *Theory X* and *Theory Y*. The former states that workers need constant outside pressure and motivation to stay on task and get the job done. According to this view, the job ranks very low among individuals' values.

On the other hand, Theory Y says that people may be ambitious and self-determined because they engage in work that satisfies their higher-ranking values. Under Theory X, employees require a lot of incentives, rewards, and encouragement to keep them focused. Yet if the company (or person) you work for has communicated your role in terms of your highest values, then you automatically become self-reliant and more productive. From this perspective, you can have greater freedom, job satisfaction, and a sense of purpose in your day-to-day activities.

Indeed, the only real difference between needing outside motivation and being self-determined is the degree to which you've linked your job role and all of the different components of that role to your highest values.

The more you can fulfill your values by making as many links as possible, the more your productivity, dedication, inspiration, and loyalty to your job will increase. You will be eager to learn and will dedicate yourself to achieving great results. You'll end up asking your employer for more responsibility because you love what you do, and you get it done quickly. Others will rely on you and trust your work. Linking your job to your values will empower your life in all areas, and you won't run out of opportunities to do what truly inspires you.

Plumbing Is a Rock Star's Job

I know a very successful businesswoman who owns a plumbing company that primarily serves a wealthy clientele (a business similar to the one my dad owned when I was growing up). She called me one day some years ago for advice on a challenge she was facing. One of her longtime clients had asked if his son could work for her. She hesitated at first, but then agreed to put him on the payroll because she needed someone to help out in the stockroom. Not long after she hired him, though, she was regretting her decision.

Although the client's 21-year-old son showed up every day, he clearly didn't want to be there. He wore headphones and listened to music all day instead of paying attention to his work. It turns out that his father thought it was time for his son to have some responsibility and earn his own money, so the young man took the job to satisfy his dad.

Now my friend was in a bind because she was stuck with an employee who was slacking off. She didn't want to fire him because she was afraid of losing a good client, but she knew that things couldn't continue as they were because her business would eventually suffer.

After filling me in on the details, she asked, "Is there any way you can help him see the value of working and get him to be more productive?"

Yes, there was, I told her and asked her to have the young man come see me.

So this young man stopped by my office, and we spent two hours together. After chatting for a bit, I asked him what his life dream was. Clearly, it wasn't plumbing.

"I want to be a star, man! I want to be the lead guitarist in a rock-and-roll band."

"Well, you certainly look the part. And right now, you're stuck in that stockroom all day and you're bored, right?"

"Yeah. It's, like, a summer job. My music comes first."

"I get it. Meanwhile, though, your boss asked me to help you become more inspired by your work."

He smirked. "I can probably see why."

"So, would you like to do that? You still have to log in the hours every day, so don't you think you might as well make the most of it?"

He agreed that would be a good idea.

I asked him, "How is doing what you're doing right now going to help you become a great guitarist?"

"Stacking boxes?"

I nodded my head, and he wondered aloud, "Uh . . . is it related?"

I assured him that all things in the Universe are related.

"That sounds kind of neat—like, everything's connected and stuff—but I don't understand."

"Well, how could stacking and carrying boxes help you in the music world?"

He gave me a blank look, so I offered, "Is it possible that when you're onstage for three hours during a concert, whaling on your guitar the whole time, you'd need substantial upper-body strength? Wouldn't you say that's accurate?"

"Oh, yeah. I see. Lifting boxes does make me feel stronger, and that would help me play for longer periods."

"If you're stronger, aren't you going to be able to play more effectively and possibly with greater dexterity?"

"Sure. That makes sense."

"You know, the lady you work for is very successful, and she hangs out with a lot of very wealthy people. Is it probable that rock stars are wealthy, too?" His eyes lit up. "Do you think that your boss might actually have a connection to the music world?" He nodded. "Do you think you might actually be shipping boxes to wealthy people's homes, people who may know or work with some of those rock stars, even when you don't realize it?"

"I never thought about that!"

"Do you see that your boss is paying me handsomely to converse with you?" He nodded again, and I could see that he was really catching on now. So I continued, asking, "Can you see that she cares enough about you to make sure that you realize your dreams, in addition to helping her company?"

"Yeah, man, it does seem like that. Do you think that she might actually introduce me to people in the industry or someone who has a connection?"

Now he was thinking. So I suggested, "Why don't you ask her? What if you found out that she does have a connection? If you were more inspired about your work and contributed to her business, don't you think she would introduce you? What if working for her could open doors and create amazing opportunities for you?"

I kept on linking his job duties to his highest values until this young man was brought to inspired tears and exclaimed, "Man, I never saw the possibilities that were sitting right in front of me!"

"Everything you're looking for is surrounding you, but you have to open your eyes, and you can't be too caught up in what you think it's supposed to look like."

Less than two weeks later, I received a letter from the woman, thanking me for what I'd done. "I don't know what happened, and I don't want to try to figure it out, but thank you," she wrote. "I want to help him even more now, because he's genuinely helping me."

The young man was working from a different perspective and was grateful for the opportunities in his job. Because he began appreciating and caring about his work, the woman went out of her way to assist him in getting what he wanted in his life.

When you appreciate and care about your responsibilities, you put more of your heart and soul into what you do. And the more you put your heart into it, the more opportunities come out of it. Every time you see the correlation between what you're doing on a daily basis and how it fulfills your most inspiring dream, you move one step closer to fulfilling your purpose—just by living your life and doing your job each day.

It's wise to open your heart and mind and ask yourself, *How is whatever I'm doing assisting me in fulfilling my highest values and achieving my dream?* If you ask a quality question like this, it will lead you to a quality life. On the other hand, if you keep asking, *Why is this always happening to me?* and affirming *This sucks!* then you'll continue to manifest that reality. Whenever you think you're doing something desperate, stop and ask yourself how that particular activity is helping you reach your highest values. By doing so, you'll be more likely to love what you do and less likely to need a vacation to escape your everyday life.

Vacations in Vocation

You're more likely to require and desire vacations away from your job, career, or studies when you're uninspired about what you do. You'll want a break from whatever you perceive to be low on your values. A vacation seems necessary when you feel that you're requiring outside motivation to get you to do the tasks that go against your heart's desire.

Vacation is assumed to release the pressure from having to repeatedly do something that you don't love. This is why so many people who aren't inspired about their vocation (that is, they're not doing what they love) view vacations as an escape. Time off is set up for the majority of society who haven't taken the time to see that whatever they're doing in their daily work is assisting them in achieving what is highest among their values.

When you're truly inspired by your career, you don't think so much in terms of vacation time or holidays. Resting is wise to assist you in fulfilling your purpose, but if you're focusing on your highest values and setting inspiring goals that are in alignment, then there's less of a reason to need a break or want to run away from your responsibilities because you're inspired about what you do. People around the world ask me when I take time off from teaching and speaking, and I tell them that my vocation is my vacation because I'm inspired by my destiny.

A few years ago, I presented The Breakthrough Experience weekend program in Kingston, Ontario. A head professor from Harvard Business School was one of the attendants, and on Sunday night after the seminar, this man and I had dinner together. He was quite intelligent and definitely an eloquent communicator. He told me that I reminded him of one of his colleagues, a Nobel Prize winner whose office was just down the hall from his own.

The professor explained that if you leave campus around 6 or 7 in the evening (when it's already dark during wintertime in Boston), you'll notice that around 85 percent of the office lights are turned off because all of the staff members have gone home. If you were to return around 9 at night, you'd notice only a dozen or so lights still on. By midnight, only a few lights would be on—half a dozen at the most. If you were there around 1 or 2 in the morning, perhaps one or two lights would still be burning bright.

Those remaining lights will lead you to the offices of the Nobel Prize winners, who are alert and alive, doing what they love doing. These individuals are the ones who rise up and enlighten others in their chosen fields. People who are inspired about what they do will find their everyday tasks inspiring, and they'll often identify themselves by what they genuinely love doing. They have the energy to work longer hours; in fact, they often feel that they've hardly worked a day in their lives.

Linking Your Job to Your Highest Values

Since it's not what happens to you but how you perceive it that counts, the key to doing what you love and loving what you do is to take everything that is uninspiring about your current job (or role) and see how it helps you fulfill what *is* most important to you. If you aren't yet able to delegate an uninspiring task, then it's wise to ask how it serves you and love what you're doing anyway. If you don't, the task could become deadweight on your shoulders. Remember that when you find out how everything you don't love doing still helps you achieve your dream, you can become grateful for the work and even become inspired by it.

Every single job or experience offers something of value. It will provide you with a new skill or contact, more patience, or even more assertiveness (or humility). Something does come out of it that you can be grateful for. *Everything is linkable to everything else in the Universe.*

If you can see how each part of what you do is helping you achieve your long-term goals and how it is assisting you to live a more meaningful life, it will no longer be a challenge that holds you back. Instead, every task will become fuel that helps you be more productive and increases your opportunities and chances for advancement.

Linking your uninspired daily tasks to your highest values doesn't mean that you have to be where you are forever, never leaving your current position to pursue another aspect of your purpose. It would just allow you to do what you love on a daily basis and make progress toward a more fulfilling existence. By living a life of great inspiration and service, you'll experience even more amazing outcomes.

Exercise: Get Inspired!

Love What You Do

1. Make a list of every task in your current job or role. (For example, "Filing paperwork.")

2. Write your top-three values from your hierarchy next to the list of tasks. (For example, "Top-three values are education, family, and finances.")

3. Write a minimum of 30 ways showing how each task helps you fulfill your top values. (For example, "I learned how to structure my studying so that I became more productive, which improved my test results. I became more organized and had more time to spend with my family. I learned skills on how to file invoices and receipts for future reference.") Be sure to make at least 30 links for each of your top values. The more connections you make, the more inspired you'll feel about your job.

Do What You Love

As a human behavioral specialist and international professional educator, I'm on an airplane for more than half the year and encounter many jet-lagged individuals. Often enough, I'll sit next to someone already downing a whiskey and commenting on the downsides of air travel. At some point I'll almost always hear, "So, do you fly much?"

When I reveal that I fly about half a million miles a year, the person usually says, "Well, I don't know how you do it!"

I know that this is all a matter of perception, so I have a number of skits to employ whenever I fly. I'm either the first person on the plane so that I can have fun assisting other people, or I'm the last one on board so that I can make an entrance. Either way, I win! I walk down the aisle like a politician, waving at folks, pretending that I know them. When I get to my seat, I press the attendant call button as often as I please. After all, it's the only place where I can actually press a button, and within seconds someone (usually a beautiful woman) arrives to get me whatever I need. I have a video service on my laptop so that I can watch whatever movies I'm interested in, along with an application that displays what's happening in the world. With Internet available on more airlines, I now have a midair office. I also have headsets for any music I love.

I also imagine that I'm hosting a party on the plane, and nobody ever leaves early. Likewise, I pretend I'm doing a seminar—and what do you know? Not one person has left any of my inflight programs. I often say that the Universe is my playground, the world is my home, and every country is another room in my house. Turning something that can seem draining and uninteresting into something that is invigorating and meaningful is the difference between an uninspiring life and one where you love what you do and come alive at the chance to take on your challenges and pursue your purpose.

Deep inside, you do desire to work in a job or vocation or provide a service that you genuinely love. According to your highest values, you know the way in which you'd love to serve or help others. It's wise to complete the previous linking process I've demonstrated every three months (no matter what role you're employed in and whether you're working for yourself or someone else) to discover how every task that you do on a daily basis is assisting you in fulfilling your highest value-driven destiny.

When you see how whatever you're doing is connected to your purpose, you begin to do what you love and love what you do. You increase your certainty regarding your future direction and experience more physical vitality every day of your life.

Inspired Insights

- When you can't see a direct link between what you're currently doing and your highest values, you'll hesitate, procrastinate, become frustrated (or frustrate others), and find excuses not to continue whatever you're doing.

- By doing what you love and loving what you do, you become inspired to serve and deliver, regardless of the job or task you're doing.

- Deep within, you have the desire to expand your potential and discover how everything you do is fueling you so you can create a magnificent life.

Words of Power

Choose at least one of the following affirmations and repeat it to yourself every day for at least the next month (ideally for the next few months). If this seems particularly challenging (or particularly rewarding), make a commitment to repeat it to yourself every day for the rest of your life.

I do what I love, I love what I do, and I am handsomely and beautifully rewarded for it.

I clearly see how everyday tasks are helping me fulfill my purpose.

*I am a self-determined individual who is
inspired from within to do what I love.*

*I am a master of transforming my perception,
and I can see how everything serves.*

CHAPTER 15

Master-Planning Your Life

"We think in generalities, but we live in detail."
— **Alfred North Whitehead**

It's revitalizing to allow yourself to be, do, and have the things you love. Planning all areas of your life in ever-finer detail is an essential process toward achieving your goals and fulfilling your dreams. Know that any detail you leave out will be filled in by someone else. In fact, the obstacles you encounter along your journey are directly proportionate to the parts of your vision you've left unclear or incomplete.

For example, if I'm going to speak before an audience and I can see the entire program in my mind in advance—including all of the challenges and concerns that people may have and the solutions to those issues—then my presentation runs smoothly. Figuring out potential obstacles (and resolving them) ultimately assists me in becoming clearer on how I'd love each part of my life to be.

The master believes in his or her vision in advance, even before seeing it in physical form. It's important to take the time to really articulate and visualize how you'd love to experience all areas of your life. Whenever you would love to achieve something, it's wise to know the details—that is, *how* exactly you go from where you are now to where you would love to be. The more specific your plan of action is, the more clarity and certainty you'll have about how to reach your goal. Remember that when your goals and highest values are aligned, your mind becomes sharper and your creativity soars. You're able to see all obstacles or challenges ahead of time, and you're prepared to take action. If you write down your visions, callings, and feelings (and attach realistic time frames to each action step), you'll feel more strongly called into action to achieve your goals. Spend your time planning, visualizing, and affirming how you'd love all aspects of your life to be. Master-planning will assist you in staying focused on your highest values.

Exercise: Get Inspired!

Creating Your Master Plan for Life

Open a new document on your computer (or take out your journal) and begin creating your master plan. Take time to write out the ever-finer details of how you'd love all seven areas of your life to be. Format your plan in a way that will allow you to easily refine or revise parts of it, as this is something you'll work on throughout your life. What follows are a few samples of individual plans in the seven areas.

Spiritual

1. What would you love to *be* spiritually? (For example, "World-renowned teacher and doctor.")

2. What would you love to *do* to make this true? (For example, "Learn about different methods of healing; complete my specialized education; open a practice in the city;

assist people in healing; write books about my work; teach others.")

3. What would you love to *have* in return for this? (For example, "Extensive knowledge and appreciation of the human body; amazing results in healing; financial freedom; vocational status around the world.")

Mental

1. What would you love to *be* mentally? (For example, "A geopolitical expert.")

2. What would you love to *do* to make this true? (For example, "Gain experience in the field by traveling abroad; study at a major international university.")

3. What would you love to *have* in exchange? (For example, "Recognition of my expertise; opportunities to contribute my own theories at international summits.")

Vocational

1. What would you love to *be* vocationally? (For example, "A featured performer in a major dance troupe.")

2. What would you love to *do* to make this true? (For example, "Develop my talent at the local level; work my way up to the junior corps de ballet; advance to a prominent ensemble.")

3. What would you love to *have* in exchange? (For example, "The applause of an enthusiastic audience; performances

choreographed specifically for me; a partner who's as inspired about dance as I am.")

Financial

1. What would you love to *be* financially? (For example, "A philanthropist who 'reverse tithes' like Sir John Templeton did.")

2. What would you love to *do* to make this true? (For example, "Master the principles of investing.")

3. What would you love to *have* in exchange? (For example, "An investment account with a balance in excess of $1 billion.")

Familial

1. What would you love to *be* in your family life? (For example, "A loving spouse and father of two children.")

2. What would you love to *do* to make this true? (For example, "Devote at least three hours a day to my children; take my family on trips to foreign countries.")

3. What would you love to *have* in exchange? (For example, "Meaningful heart-to-heart moments with my wife.")

Social

1. What would you love to *be* socially? (For example, "A master social networker.")

2. What would you love to *do* to make this true? (For example, "Become an expert in networking; attend wonderful social functions, such as benefits, to meet new and interesting people.")

3. What would you love to *have* in exchange? (For example, "Access to the movers and shakers of the world; countless memorable and inspiring experiences.")

Physical

1. What would you love to *be* physically? (For example, "A beautiful, fit runner.")

2. What would you love to *do* to make this true? (For example, "Train four hours per week.")

3. What would you love to *have* in exchange? (For example, "Energy and strength to take on any activity that inspires me.")

As you work on creating and refining your master plan, you'll notice that some of these questions are easier to answer than others. It won't be difficult to address the areas that rank high in your values hierarchy. You'll naturally possess a greater degree of clarity and certainty about how you'd love your life to be in the areas that are important to you. On the other hand, you may struggle in the areas that concern your lower values, but don't let that stop you from completing this exercise. Planning all areas will empower you and help you pursue your dreams.

If you're feeling sluggish about a specific area (a value that ranks low right now), then link it to what is most important to you (your highest values). This will allow you to discover what role it plays in your inspired destiny.

Setting Realistic Goals

Whenever you set too small of a goal for yourself, you can get bored with it. Whenever you set too big of a goal for yourself, you can get burned out by it. This "feedback" wakes you up so that you'll set more meaningful, realistic goals with reasonable time frames. Remember that when you set goals from your authentic self, you increase your ability to achieve your desired outcome.

The more strategic planning you employ, the more realistic your goals will be. You'll know how much time and energy will be devoted to fulfilling all of the steps along the way to achieving the end result. Mastering this art is essential to stay focused and on track.

Exercise: Get Inspired!

"Chunk Down" Your Goals

It's wise to "chunk down" (that is, break up) large and difficult projects or objectives into smaller, more manageable tasks, linking each one to your higher values. Doing so prevents you from becoming overwhelmed and doubting whether you'll be able to achieve your goals. You'll feel much less stressed out and scattered when you know exactly where to start and where to go once you're on a roll.

For example, let's say you wish to share your inspiring message with the world, and your goal is to write an 80,000-word book. To chunk it down, you might do the following:

1. Identify about ten high-priority ideas that you'll communicate in the book.

2. List the subjects in the order you think they should be presented, and then number them. These are your chapter topics.

3. For each one of the chapter ideas, identify seven high-priority sub-ideas you'll further explore. List them in the order you think is most logical and flows best. This gives you a rough outline of the contents of each chapter.

4. For each chapter's seven main topics, list seven elements that support them, including real-life examples and personal experiences, quotations, reasoning, explanation, references to pop culture or other books, and so on. This offers you a sense of what to include in each of the sections that make up a whole chapter.

5. Now you can really begin to write. Examine the first sub-idea within Chapter One, and write seven sentences summarizing that thought. Continue to write a paragraph for each of the seven supporting elements (each paragraph consisting of four to seven sentences). Then move on to the next sub-idea and do the same thing (and then the next, and the next, and so on).

6. When you've finished writing material for all of your chapters, their sub-ideas, and the supporting elements, you'll have your first draft!

By chunking a project down like this, you make your outcome much simpler and more realistic to achieve. You dissolve the stress and pressure that you have on yourself to create results in unrealistic time frames.

Creating What You Would Love

Whenever you're writing about how you'd love your life to be in all seven areas, imagine yourself ten years into the future and think about what you would love to be doing. What would be truly inspiring? Visualize precisely how you'd love your life to be, and write down the images you see in your mind's eye. Master-plan your future as if it were already in existence. Make sure that everything you write in your master plan is deeply meaningful to you.

You can use your master plan to write out your goals and how you'll go about achieving them, including intermediate steps to ensure that you stay on track. I've been master-planning my life for nearly four decades, and I have several volumes that outline in fine detail how I'd love my life to be across all seven areas on all levels. My master plan is one of the most powerful tools that I've utilized in achieving the goals that I've reached, as well as for those greater achievements I'm aiming for into the future.

Inspired Insights

- It's revitalizing to allow yourself to be, do, and have the things that you love in life.

- Master planners believe in their vision long before they see it manifesting in physical form.

- Any detail that you leave out of your master plan may become an obstacle on the path to achieving your dream.

- The more details you can outline about your goals, the more realistic your goals will be.

- Your master plan will be one of the most powerful tools you can use to create the life you would love.

Words of Power

Choose at least one of the following affirmations and repeat it to yourself every day for at least the next month (ideally for the next few months). If this seems particularly challenging (or particularly rewarding), make a commitment to repeat it to yourself every day for the rest of your life.

I set realistic, meaningful goals that inspire me.

*I am a master of creating goals that
perfectly align with my highest values.*

I master-plan my life in ever-finer detail.

I chunk down big tasks into smaller, manageable actions.

CHAPTER 16

How to Create What You Would Love

"Somehow I can't believe that there are any heights that can't be scaled by a man who knows the secrets of making dreams come true."
— **Walt Disney**

For more than three decades, I've shared how I've realized my dream to live an inspired life with thousands of people worldwide. Now it's your turn. Let's explore some key elements that will assist you in manifesting what you love so that you can achieve *your* dreams.

Be sure to take the insights here and apply them to your own life. Experience the power you have—through your own mind *and* body—to reach whatever you're aspiring to.

Focus on What You Would Love to Create

It's essential to concentrate upon the things that you'd love to be, do, and have in life. When I was filmed for my part in *The Secret* (a film devoted to the "how" of manifesting one's dreams), I emphasized that your innermost dominant thought becomes your outermost tangible reality. In other words, you'll move your life in the direction of what is most on your mind.

Since you're always thinking about *something,* it is wise to consciously focus your thoughts upon how you can live according to your highest values. Fill your mind with what is most important to you, and tap into the inspiring thoughts and ideas that you would love to bring into reality. Note that whenever you think about activities that are associated with your lower values (unless you're planning ways to delegate them or linking them to your highest values), they can become frustrating boulders that seem to momentarily block your path.

When your goals are aligned with your highest values, and what you'd love to achieve absolutely reflects your authentic self, then you'll automatically think about those goals. When you're grateful for your challenges, for yourself, and for those around you—and you're appreciative for the way it is—you have the power to create and shape the seven areas of life. (Refer to Chapter 4 for a refresher of the seven areas of life.) To put it simply, you bring about what you think and "thank" about.

Visualize *What You Would Love to Create*

Visualize yourself fulfilling your purpose; do it three times a day, if possible. See yourself doing what you love across all seven areas of life to add more depth to your vision. The longer you can stay focused on your inspiring picture, the more you increase the probability of manifesting it. When you hold your vision in your mind's eye and see yourself acting out in detail your desired outcome, you build momentum. Be sure to tune in to your desired outcome instead of the doubts, challenges, or other problems you might be facing on your journey.

Begin by filling in the details of your master plan and center your innermost thoughts upon that. Remember that the more you visualize, the more likely it is that you will experience it in your reality. The success you achieve will be directly proportional to the vividness of your inspiring vision.

Affirm What You Would Love to Create

Everything you say has an impact. When you repeat something over and over again, either to yourself or to others, it becomes part of who you are. _You begin to believe it._ You can tap into this tremendous power by writing and reciting concise and meaningful statements about your ability to achieve your inspired destiny.

Throughout this book, you've been reading (and, I hope, affirming) the many "Words of Power" found at the end of each chapter. If you haven't already done so, choose two or three affirmations that resonate with you, and plan on saying them to yourself for the rest of your life. You're welcome to use the ones I've provided here, perhaps revising them so that they're more personal, or make up new ones altogether. The important thing is that you choose words that confirm the truth of your vision and ability to fulfill it. Make sure that your affirmations are in the present tense and that they align with your highest values. Take it from me—what started out as uplifting words actually manifested into the life of my dreams.

Feel What You Would Love to Create

When you _think_ about fulfilling your highest values, you'll be inspired. And when you _feel_ inspired, you increase your ability to create or uncover opportunities that will help you achieve your goals. With this powerful outlook, you not only impact every aspect of your life, but you also affect the rest of the world.

There are four primary feelings that assist you in living your dream. They emerge when you tune in to your inner wisdom and maintain harmony with your highest values. They are as follows:

183

1. *Gratitude.* Gratitude is the gateway to the heart that allows your authentic self to radiate outward to those around you. It is a genuine appreciation of yourself, other people, and the world. When you feel grateful for what you have, you'll receive more of what you love and the power to transform your life.

2. *Unconditional love.* Unconditional love is having an open heart and no desire to change yourself or others. You feel content about your life and the Universe as it is. It is a poised, present, powerful, and patient state of heart and soul.

3. *Inspiration.* Inspiration is an expression of living according to your highest values. When you're focused on fulfilling what is important to you, it's nearly impossible not to live a purposeful and meaningful life. People naturally desire to be in your company when you are inspired and love what you do.

4. *Enthusiasm.* Everyone loves to be served by and in the company of people who are enthusiastic about what they do. Enthusiasm is a magnetic feeling that will give you incredible influence in your social circles, workplace, family environment, and other areas of life.

When you embrace these feelings, your body and mind will be in harmony, and you'll increase your ability to attract and/or create your desired outcome. Every cell in your body will experience an accompanying state of certainty, presence, inspiration, and gratitude. Remember, you feel that "you can" when you're aligned with your highest values, and believe that "you can't" when you are not. Doubt comes about when you're pursuing something that is low on your values list.

Your self-confidence correlates to how you're feeling, and of course, how you feel impacts what you focus on and ultimately manifest. Your self-image decides your destiny! Concentrate on these four powerful feelings throughout the day, and nothing can stop you from achieving your dreams.

Write about What You Would Love to Create

An important part of master-planning, physically writing down or typing out your aspirations in life, will assist you in turning them into reality. When you do so, you're making a commitment to act on them. A short pencil is better than a long memory when it comes to manifesting your ideas. This process makes your goals much more achievable.

Regularly review your master plan of what you would love to be, do, and have in all seven areas of your life and refine it as needed. Update and rewrite it, and add details as you become clearer on your inspired destiny. Writing down what you would love organizes your thoughts so that you can develop an action plan to help you achieve your desired outcome.

Act on What You Would Love to Create

Because you perceive your world through your individual hierarchy of values, you judge and label the people, places, and events you encounter accordingly. When you view things from a one-sided perspective, you end up reacting emotionally to the circumstances in your environment, but when you tune in to your balanced soul, you act from inspiration. Inspired action is more powerful than emotional reaction. In this state, you are empowered and in control. Whenever you take action when you're inspired, you bring order to the chaos that may appear to surround you.

Every morning, take some time to stop and sit. Get quiet and ask your inner, most authentic self for guidance that will help you fulfill your purpose. Define seven high-priority action steps for that day. Write them down and then tackle them in order of importance. When you do so, your self-worth increases; when you don't, it tends to fall. Remember to focus on the _ABC_'s instead of the _XYZ_'s. Your high-priority actions will be the ones where you're providing an inspired and loving service to others and being handsomely rewarded for it. Make a habit of delivering even more value than what people are expecting.

As you're writing your seven daily action steps, ask yourself the following:

1. *What would I absolutely love to do in life?*

2. *How do I become handsomely (or beautifully) paid to do it?*

3. *What are seven steps I could complete today that would enable me to do it?*

4. *What obstacles might I run into, and how do I solve them in advance?*

5. *What worked or didn't work before that I can incorporate or avoid today?*

6. *How can I do what I love more efficiently and effectively?*

7. *How did whatever I experienced today (whether it was positive or negative) serve me in fulfilling my highest values?*

Remember that the quality of your life is based on the quality of the questions you ask yourself, as well as the quality and quantity of the actions you take. Every day, inquire about and act on what you'd love to achieve in life.

<u>Materialize</u> *What You Would Love to Create*

Some theologians and scientists believe that intelligent thoughts and creative ideas give rise to all of the material substances and forms within the Universe. In other words, all tangible, visible manifestations are the result of willful intention. Everything that is currently in physical form also has a metaphysical element underlying it—one that is formless and intangible. We bring objects into form by focusing upon them either through metaphysical inductions or physical actions.

The Universe is passively waiting for your clearly defined, dominant thoughts about how you'd love your life to be. Open yourself up to the infinite possibilities. Everything you need to create what you would most love to experience is available to you in the present moment. Live your life with such inner certainty that everything you dream materializes into the form you'd love most.

Energize **What You Would Love to Create**

Energy is infinite and available to everything and everyone in the Universe. When you breathe, your diaphragm gives you the ability to capture and transform this energy into creative actions or thoughts. That's right: a deep inhale fills you with the full energy of your life.

Think about it. Physical life begins with the first breath and ends with the last. The quality and quantity of the energy you receive, transform, and generate are a reflection of your breathing patterns. As your breath wanders, so does your mind. As your mind wanders, so does your breath. Lopsided breathing will stir your mind into thinking about and focusing upon the past or future. Balanced breathing will bring poise, presence, and power to your body and mind.

You'll notice that your breathing patterns change throughout the day when you're doing different activities of higher or lower priority, and when you perceive yourself to be more supported than challenged or more challenged than supported. Longer inhalations and shorter exhalations wake you up and make you feel more excited or elated. Longer exhalations and shorter inhalations put you to sleep and make you feel more subdued or even depressed. When your breathing is even, however, you become present, certain, and poised; and you're in your most powerful state of being.

Exercise: Get Inspired!

Balance Your Breathing

1. Find a place where you can sit still and get quiet. Settle in.

2. Breathing through your nose, inhale to the count of seven.

3. Hold your breath comfortably for seven seconds.

4. Breathing through your nose, exhale to the count of seven.

5. Hold your breath comfortably for seven seconds.

6. Repeat the previous steps until your breathing naturally equilibrates (or for at least seven rounds).

As you're doing the above exercise, consider alternating cycles by balancing longer breaths (greater than seven seconds or counts) with shorter breaths (less than seven seconds or counts). Inhale for a length equal to your exhale. The bottom line is that when you breathe evenly, you'll become more present and focused on taking inspired, high-priority actions toward achieving your intended outcomes.

Be Grateful for What You Love

Keep in mind that the more gratitude you feel, the more likely you will experience events to be grateful for. This is so vital that I'd like to quickly touch on this trait again. You become genuinely appreciative when you're able to embrace the perfect balance of benefits and drawbacks, pleasures and pains, supports and challenges, and positives and negatives in each moment throughout your life. Even your most inspiring dreams will provide this perfect balance of opposites. When you appreciate yourself, other people, and the world as they are, you momentarily stop trying to disown half of your own or other people's traits.

Every time you have gratitude for what you love, you increase your capacity to manifest new opportunities and resources to fulfill your inspired destiny. You become poised and certain, and you're firmly in the present instead of focusing on something that happened in the past or that may or may not happen in the future. You feel the energy required to take actions toward creating what you would love. Your authentic self is your most efficient state for living a purpose-filled existence. Gratitude is the essence of your existence.

You Deserve What You Love

You deserve all the things that you'd truly love to experience in life. You value yourself most when you embrace both sides of your being: nice and mean, generous and greedy, and so on. Variations in your self-esteem correlate directly with your emotional states. You grow every time you're grateful for yourself and your life as it is—without any desire for change. How much you value yourself is determined by examining all seven areas of your life.

Feeling guilty about the things that you have (or haven't) done in the past can distract you and may even prevent you from feeling that you are fulfilling your purpose. It's wise to dissolve your guilt and regrets. When you do, you'll also let go of unfair and compensatory exchanges you may have felt were necessary. When you do what you love and love what you do, you experience an elevated feeling of your worth. You deserve to receive what you'd love.

What You Say to Yourself Impacts Your Destiny

What you think about, visualize, feel strongly about, write about, and talk about has an impact on your life. As I've mentioned, when I was 17, Paul Bragg shared an affirmation with me that I've since repeated thousands of times in my mind (and a few times in this book): *I am a genius, and I apply my wisdom.* Back then, I didn't understand the power of self-dialogue, but today I know that one simple affirmation absolutely changed my life.

Earlier in this book, I told you about the time I was tutoring some students during college, and one of my peers whispered, "That Demartini is a friggin' genius." But I didn't tell you what happened next. That night after I heard that echo of my affirmation, I decided that I was going to fill my mind with thoughts and statements that aligned exactly with how I wanted my life to be.

I sat down at my desk for several hours and wrote inspiring statements for myself to memorize and recite whenever I had a spare moment. This is what I came up with:

> *I am a master of persistence, and I do what it takes to achieve my goals. I am a master of comprehension and retain everything I read. I have a photographic mind and a vivid memory. I am a master moneymaker, and whatever I touch turns to gold. I am always at the right place at the right time to meet the right people to make the right deal. I travel whatever distance and pay whatever price is necessary to provide my service of love to the world. People are willing to travel whatever distance and pay whatever price to receive my service of love.*

Today all of these affirmations have proven true—they accurately describe my life. Remember that when what you say to yourself has great meaning for you and is aligned with your highest values, it will directly increase your ability to manifest what you love.

Inspired Insights

- Focus your thoughts and visualizations on the things that are most inspiring to you.

- Embrace and enhance the four feelings that assist you in creating what you'd love: gratitude, unconditional love, inspiration, and enthusiasm.

- The Universe is waiting for you to actively live your inspired destiny.

- When you are grateful for what you have, you get even more to be grateful for.

- You deserve to create and experience a magnificent life.

Words of Power

Choose at least one of the following affirmations and repeat it to yourself every day for at least the next month (ideally for the next few months). If this seems particularly challenging (or particularly rewarding), make a commitment to repeat it to yourself every day for the rest of your life.

Whatever I think and thank about, I bring about.

I deserve to be, do, and have the things that most inspire me.

I balance my breathing and act on what I love.

I stay focused on my high-priority action steps.

PART III

LIFE INSIGHTS

CHAPTER 17

Having an
Astronomical Vision

*"The sense of paralysis proceeds not so much out of the mammoth
size of the problem but out of the puniness of the purpose."*
— **Norman Cousins**

When what you envision and hear inside of you overcome all
the opinions and reactions outside of you, you've begun to master
your life. Having an astronomical vision to dedicate yourself to is
the most effective way to empower all seven areas of your life and
fulfill your inspired destiny. The magnitude of your master plan
determines how much of an impact it's going to have.

This is how it works: If you want to make a difference in yourself, you have to have a vision at least as big as your family. If
you want to make a difference in your family, you have to have
a vision at least as big as your community. If you want to make a
difference in your community, you have to have a vision at least
as big as your city. If you want to make a difference in your city,
you have to have a vision at least as big as your state. If you want
to make a difference in your state, you have to have a vision as big
as your nation. If you want to make a national impact, you have

to have a global vision; and if you want to touch the world and leave an immortal legacy, then you have to have an astronomical, soul-inspired vision.

What Is Your Vision?

Your innermost self constantly urges you to expand to ever-greater circles of influence, intellect, insight, and inspiration. Your soul, the immortal part of you, takes you beyond where you are today and into a celestial vision for your life—possibly even into your legacy of the afterlife. Remember that your vision is made up of the images you focus upon that convey how you would love your life to be. You may envision the things that you'd love to do, experiences you'd love to have, people you'd love to associate with, opportunities you'd love to pursue, and the difference you'd love to make as you lead a meaningful, inspired life.

Your astronomical vision is captured in the essence of your highest values. You focus your innermost thoughts on your vision; you feel it in your heart; and you talk about it, dream about it, and see it daily in your mind's eye, consciously or unconsciously. It will always reflect what is most important to you. Your tears of gratitude and inspiration are signs that you've captured your astronomical vision, your unique life purpose.

This is who you really are, as it comes directly from your heart. When you're in touch with your authentic self, you tap into the power that fuels you and helps you reach your goals.

The Power of Your Astronomical Vision

Your astronomical vision possesses phenomenal power, and amazing things can happen when you're determined to follow it. All sorts of obstacles simply evaporate the moment your picture becomes clear and certain.

Here's a personal example about the power of a vision: In early fall 1982, I was in Houston studying comparative religion and philosophy and working on a book titled *The Tree of Life*. One night, I was up late reading. Around two in the morning, I'd just finished another book in the 72-volume series of the Vedic texts when I stopped to do a meditation. As I settled my mind and tuned in to my inner voice, I saw an inspiring vision and heard a short message: *And they came the world over.*

In my vision, I saw the year 2054, where thousands of students were coming from every country around the globe to study my teachings and become a part of my service. In that moment, I envisioned a comprehensive, advanced curriculum that would expand my students' minds and open their hearts to the hidden order that I inwardly sensed was underlying all of existence. For the next five hours, I created an outline of 300 courses that I felt deeply inspired from within to present to people as part of my life purpose. I captured that vision and wrote down everything so that I'd remember the power of what I'd heard and witnessed that night.

Just a few weeks later, I presented the first of a series of new classes to 27 of the most aware individuals who I felt would best represent my initial "students of wisdom." The group was made up of doctors, theologians, artists, musicians, chemists, physicists, entrepreneurs, and many others. My first class included a three-hour guided-imagery meditation that took us on a journey from where we were in the room to the imagined macroworld of the astronomical Universe, and then to the imagined microworld of the subatomic Universe.

Since then, I've received deeply inspired, lucid images on how I'd love my life to be and what I'd ultimately love to pursue. I've seen and heard inner visions and messages nearly every day that have guided me to continue taking action toward my destiny. I've been persistently growing my resources, my influence, and the outreach of my courses over the years. I've now taught in more than 60 countries and reached people in more than 134. Today, most of what I saw in my mind's eye has either come true or is in the process of being realized. I know that it's my mission to share what is in my heart, and I've stayed true to the visions and messages as they came to me late that night.

My point is this: *never* underestimate the power of having a vision that exceeds your current environment and/or circumstances. Remember that when your voice and vision on the inside are more profound than all of the opinions you're subjected to on the outside, you've begun to master your life. Today, my vision helps me live a magnificent life, and you deserve the same.

How a Vision Assists You Every Day

I often say that whoever has the most certainty rules the game. Clarifying your vision increases your certainty tenfold. Having an astronomical vision for what you'd ultimately love to achieve gives you the perspective to look back at the earth and recognize it as a playground where you can create amazing experiences.

You'll be given an entirely different perspective and paradigm for living, and you'll transcend the challenges that appear to stand in the way of you fulfilling your mission. Your inspiring vision will significantly enhance your ability to make a difference and influence those around you. It will transform the way you interact with others, and you'll begin to engage in an entirely different level of conversation. You'll start to associate with the individuals who can assist you in expanding your vision even further.

By discovering your astronomical vision, you'll attract even more opportunities. Your strong sense of purpose, presence, and gratitude will increase as you pursue what you love. An astronomical vision will forever transform the way in which you see yourself, inspiring you from within to go for what is most important to you. Staying true to yourself will keep you on track to fulfilling your purpose, maximizing your goals, and achieving your most inspiring dreams.

When your astronomical vision is alive and present, it's no longer out there in the future—it's in the here-and-now. It's your destiny, and you'll fulfill what you appeared here on Earth to do. Take the time to become crystal clear and feel inspired in the pursuit of a cause greater than your everyday mortal life.

Follow in the Footsteps of Your Vision

As you know, I've been following my dream of being one of the world's greatest educators and philosophers since I was 17 years old. I began tutoring way back when I was attending college myself, and by the time I went on to professional school, I was teaching classes nearly every day or night to whoever wanted to listen. It kept growing from there, and it never stopped.

I moved through the different magnitudes of my vision—that is, through the community and city, then on to the state and nation, and now I teach all over the world year-round. It would be impossible to convince me that a person with an astronomical vision can't eventually create a global effect. Remember that many of the greatest minds in history constructed inspiring legacies through the power of their vision.

Once you're clear on the ever-finer details of *your* astronomical vision, don't let anyone distract you. Remain steady on the inside among the many seeming adversities and challenges. Care about yourself and others, and stay true to what is in your heart.

When I was living near San Diego about 20 years ago, I had the opportunity to visit the Self-Realization Fellowship center, which was established by Paramahansa Yogananda in 1937. Yogananda was one of Mahatma Gandhi's teachers, a mystic who educated people on many topics from the science of breath to the science of meditation. When I visited the center, I spoke to an elderly woman who managed it. She told me about the history of Yogananda and the hundreds of temples and centers he had built throughout the world. When I asked how he was able to accomplish so much, the woman explained, "When people met Yogananda, as I did many years ago, they were drawn to his presence. They were drawn into his vision; they were drawn by his inspiration. He saw his life purpose so clearly that others wanted to participate. People came from all walks of life and offered to contribute in some way. Whether it was donating their time or money, they wanted to participate and help carry out his vision."

This allowed Yogananda to continue spreading his teachings across the planet, and he was fueled by staying true to his inspired vision. When you discover your astronomical vision, whatever that may be, you will feel this same power take hold of you. It will continue to grow, inspiring you to pursue your purpose and achieve great things.

Your Vision Keeps You Growing

Whenever your vision becomes clouded or you momentarily lose sight of your goal, you've probably just hit a plateau. You may temporarily feel uninspired to take action toward any outcome. Anytime you lose sight of your soul purpose, it's time to get back in touch with the real reason for doing what you do. And remember that your true inspiration is your highest value. You'll feel that your life lacks purpose if you start to succumb to outer influences instead of listening to your inner voice. Honor your authentic hierarchy of values instead of accepting the values of those you feel inferior to. Unlock your talents and genius. Dig deep and rediscover your astronomical vision. What do you see? What do you dream of experiencing? What would you love to see come to fruition?

I once asked a great media magnate how he built his global empire, and he said, "I look down upon the earth as if from outer space, and while spinning it in my hand, I ask myself, *What message do I want to bring to what country today?*" The main point is that no matter what it is that you'd love to do, there's potential for you to have a massive impact. See all of the events in your life as leading you toward fulfilling an inspiring vision for yourself and the world, touching the lives of countless people. View your vision in such detail that you can see it vividly. (Remember that any detail you leave out can become a challenge that you might later encounter along the path.)

When you envision the profound and meaningful impact you'd love to have, you increase the probability of actually achieving your goal. To the degree to which you listen to your soul, communicate your vision, and inspire others, then the people around you will rally and help you work toward manifesting that vision in the world. Those who lose their vision perish, and those who stay true to it flourish.

Be aware that fear and guilt can hinder you from becoming crystal clear on what you'd love to contribute to the world. Balance out your mind-set, and dissolve that emotional baggage. Find out what you believe you've done (or haven't done), and remember that imbalanced emotions distract you from giving yourself permission to fulfill an extraordinary life vision. You deserve to reveal the truth in your heart and set yourself free. Place no limits on your dreams. Your soul puts no constraints on what you can achieve. Know that you're here to do something truly magnificent.

Inspired Insights

- Having an astronomical vision is a powerful key to fulfilling your inspired destiny.

- Your soul is calling you to ever-greater magnitudes of vision.

- Whenever your vision seems clouded or you feel that you've lost your purpose, you've just hit a temporary plateau in your life that when broken through will make your vision even clearer.

- Your astronomical vision will drive you to transcend any challenges so that you may live a meaningful existence.

- Your soul puts no constraints on what is possible for your life.

Words of Power

Choose at least one of the following affirmations and repeat it to yourself every day for at least the next month (ideally for the next few months). If this seems particularly challenging (or particularly rewarding), make a commitment to repeat it to yourself every day for the rest of your life.

I have an astronomical vision, and I am dedicated to
creating my life the way I would love it to be.

My astronomical vision encompasses the planet,
and I am inspired by a great cause.

I give myself permission to envision an extraordinary life for myself.

I have the inner vision of a hawk, and I can see a vast horizon.

CHAPTER 18

Expanding Your
Time Horizons

"The greatest use of a life is to spend it for something that outlasts it."
— **William James**

A gentleman named Elliott Jaques wrote a book called *Requisite Organization* in which he showed that the people who are at the very bottom of a corporation—those who are doing the most basic and redundant tasks—think in terms of hour to hour and day to day. Those who are in supervisory roles—making sure that the lower-level employees are satisfactorily doing their jobs—think in terms of day to day and week to week. The individuals who are in management positions think week to week and month to month. The people above them, who hold roles in middle management, think in terms of month to month and year to year. Those in upper management may think year to year and perhaps five years out. Finally, the CEO of the company is usually thinking from decade to decade, spanning several years.

As our "time horizons" expand, our accountability increases and so does our vision of what is possible. (A *time horizon* refers to a future point in time when something is to be done.) Our perspective of the bigger picture grows when we transcend our immediate wants and focus on the future. Those who are at the top of an organization say things like, "If we aim in this direction over the next generation, we'll grab a greater percentage of the market share." These men and women have the long-term patience to pursue a broader vision.

When you have an astronomical vision, you think in long-range terms. Know that the sage listens to that voice from within and follows his or her soul purpose. Why not follow your heart and set goals for future centuries? Successful businesspeople and entrepreneurs, such as Richard Branson, for instance, are already thinking in terms of the next millennium. Branson isn't just thinking globally; he's thinking about a plan for Earth that encompasses the whole solar system! This is the sign of a visionary. Tap into the visionary in *you,* and watch what it will do for your inspired destiny.

You Are a Visionary

Yes, you have a visionary living inside you, but you often shrink that aspect of yourself in fear of what other people will think about your stepping out and pursuing a different path. Dissolve the anxiety that's trying to stop you from taking that leap and ask yourself, *What would I love to master?* Consider the ways in which you could effect global change, leaving your mark on the world for hundreds of years to come.

Train your mind to think about your ultimate purpose over the longest amount of time you can imagine. Envision the world 50 to 100 years in the future, when you've already contributed to society and done something incredible with your life. What have you achieved? What will you be remembered for? In what ways would you love to be known for making a difference? When you pass from your physical body, what would you most love people to be saying about you?

Your Time Horizons Determine Your Achievements

The time frame that you hold within your mind determines the scale on which you're able to create and achieve. As your consciousness and level of awareness grow, your goals will also expand in length of time. When you're a child, you think in terms of hour to hour and day to day, and a week seems like an eternity. As you grow older, though, you start to think from week to week and into months. As you enter adulthood, you think in terms of month to month, year to year, and what lies beyond. Are you able to clearly see the infinite detail of your goals in five years from now? What about in ten years? Fifty years? A hundred? Five hundred?

You'll see the details in a goal that's within your current time horizon. The more aligned your goals are with your highest values, the more you achieve and the more you expand your time horizons. The more goals you realize, the more your awareness increases and the more you build your confidence. Your maturity grows as you begin to think longer and longer term. Make sure that when you set goals for yourself, you keep them within your current time horizon; when you do, you increase the probability of achieving them. But also place greater time horizons on each goal that you set so that you can further expand your mind in thinking about your ultimate objectives.

The Power of Expanding Your Time Horizons

Whenever you expand your time horizons, you decrease the probability of having lopsided emotional reactions to what occurs around you on a day-to-day basis, and you more patiently (and maturely) follow your inner vision. For example, if you're planning a picnic that will last half the day, you hardly bat an eye when something goes awry for a few seconds. But if you're planning a special dinner that will only last an hour or so, then the pressure of making every minute perfect can make you touchy about even the smallest glitch.

Keep in mind that the visionary thinks ahead in terms of years, decades, generations, centuries, and even millennia. You experience an entirely different feeling when you focus on immediate gratification as opposed to the long-term goals that come from your heart.

All those years ago, Paul Bragg taught me that we all have something we'd love to do with our life, and once we figure it out, it's wise to set goals not only for ourselves, but for our family, community, city, state, nation, world, and beyond for at least the next 100 years. I am now nearly 40 years into my visionary journey, and I'm just as inspired today as I was when I clarified my vision in 1972.

Defining your mission and setting goals for the next hundred years or so will significantly increase your certainty about your destiny. You will start to think far ahead of where you are today and no longer be caught up in the smaller daily challenges and changes along the path to fulfilling your purpose. You'll experience powerful emotional stability that allows no one to throw you off your inspired path. Let no mortals interfere with your immortal vision!

As you increase your time horizons, you may also begin transcending authority figures you once revered. Until you're about 18 years old, this role is most often filled by your parents. From 18 to about 24, it may be assumed by a college professor. Eventually, your greatest authority may become your employer or possibly the leaders of your city, state, nation, or world. You continue to transcend these different levels as you expand the horizons in your mind and give yourself permission to do something amazing. Consider this: your greatest accountability to the world is only as great as your highest authority. Remain humble only to the natural laws and intelligence of the Universe.

Value yourself enough to make sure that you're thinking as far out into the future as possible when you plan your life. Ask yourself what you'd love to be, do, and have in five years and then ten years (and keep going). Discover what impact you'd love to make on the world 100 years from now. How would you love to influence the world 500 years after you've passed away?

Know that you have an immortal legacy buried in your heart that transcends all time horizons.

Great Horizons for Your Life

Throughout history, the people who made a difference in the world have been the ones who had an immortal vision that was initially buried in their hearts. At some point, they found the courage to overcome whatever challenges stood in the way of achieving their dreams. As part of my own master plan, I've written and continue to refine my own life story. In that autobiography, I detail my achievements, awards, turning points, and defining moments that have determined (or will determine) my inspired destiny.

At the end of your life, on the last day before you pass from your physical body, you're probably going to ask yourself, *Did I do everything I could with everything that I was given?* And you want to be able to reply, *Absolutely! I stood on the shoulders of giants, and I expanded my horizons so that I could fulfill my inspired destiny.*

Your soul doesn't put a limit on how big your vision is, but your physical senses and perceptions *do.* Change the course of history and the lives of millions, if you desire. Distinguish yourself as a leader in your field rather than a follower, and do something magnificent during your lifetime. See the unlimited possibilities before you.

Inspired Insights

- The space and time horizons in your mind determine the level of conscious evolution that you have attained.

- Setting goals for 1, 5, 10, 20, 50, or even 100 years and beyond increases the power you have to create the life you would love.

- As you get older, your space and time horizons expand, and you transcend your greatest authorities to have a significant influence on the world.

- The more goals you achieve, the more your awareness increases and your confidence grows.

- Your soul doesn't put a limit on how big your vision is; your own physical senses and distorted perception of reality do.

- Value yourself enough to set goals beyond your lifetime to leave a mark in history and an immortal legacy.

- Give yourself permission to shoot for the stars and live an extraordinary, amazing life.

Words of Power

Choose at least one of the following affirmations and repeat it to yourself every day for at least the next month (ideally for the next few months). If this seems particularly challenging (or particularly rewarding), make a commitment to repeat it to yourself every day for the rest of your life.

I set goals for the short-, mid-, and long-terms—and for eternity.

I give myself permission to uncover my magnificence and leave an immortal legacy in the world.

My time horizon continues to grow because I set goals that are aligned with my highest values.

I am a visionary, and my influence touches lives everywhere I go.

CHAPTER 19

Would You Love to Be a Leader or a Follower?

"Leadership can be thought of as a capacity to define oneself to others in a way that clarifies and expands a vision of the future."
— **Edwin H. Friedman**

Throughout the ages, there have been individuals who saw things differently from the rest of the world. They had a unique vantage point and perceived possibilities and opportunities that the majority of people couldn't or wouldn't allow themselves to even imagine. As these innovative men and women spoke up, they rattled the traditions of their time and challenged cultural or societal beliefs. They first encountered resistance and sometimes opposition, but the vision they sustained themselves with eventually became self-evident, and others followed their lead. This is how the greatest achievements in history have been accomplished.

The most notable visionaries aren't typically the people who fit in; they're the ones who often speak out or act differently, seemingly marching to the beat of their own drummer. Leaders view problems or issues as potential opportunities. Perhaps they want to solve a mystery in the Universe, or maybe they're ready to tackle a question that has gone unanswered or an answer that has been unquestioned. These types of challenges awaken a *void* inside leaders that drives a *value,* which they then begin to pursue.

Genuine luminaries have original, inspired visions. They are the pioneers on the cutting edge, at the horizon of space and time in the realm of immortality. They know that they're here to fulfill their dreams and make a profound difference in the world. Over the years, the more I read about these bright stars, the more interested I was to find out whether they possess common traits. My own research findings led me to uncover seven main traits that these successful individuals demonstrate. Let's take a closer look at each one.

1. Clarifying Your Purpose, Vision, and Destiny

Having a clear purpose, vision, and destiny are signs that you're harnessing your power to create the life you'd love. Those who have changed the world were able to do so because they knew their purpose inside and out. They heeded a calling in their heart that was so strong that they refused to let any obstacle or human being stop them from fulfilling their mission on Earth.

If your vision isn't greater than the perceived challenges surrounding it, then those outside forces will win, and you'll be temporarily overruled. (Remember that any details you leave out of your master plan will be filled in by someone or something else.) Empowered people don't allow the world to dictate their destiny; they transform life as we know it by creating new trends or ideals. They aren't followers—they're bold trailblazers. In order to embrace *your* role as a leader, work on your vision every day. Visualize every possible detail and build on your action steps so that your destiny is crystal clear.

2. Maintaining Certainty about Yourself in the World

Great leaders demonstrate certainty and confidence. When you're self-assured, you attract knowledgeable people who have the skills to help you achieve your goals. You'll become dedicated to raising the standards among societies around the world in some way, shape, or form because you're certain that everyone deserves all the available resources to pursue a magnificent life. Your expanded perspective will allow you to skyrocket to even greater heights as you follow your astronomical vision.

3. Building Congruent Goals and Integrity

Leaders know to set goals that match their authentic highest values, which allow them to express order and harmony. Their presence is recognized and people are drawn to these individuals because of their integrity and order. Think of it in this way: plants grow toward the sun because they're pulled by its powerful, life-sustaining radiance. Whoever possesses the greatest order rules the game. Whoever is aligned with his or her highest values has integrity. Know that your own integrity isn't measured by what you say, but by how congruently you live with your highest values and your vision.

4. Tackling Challenges

When you get in touch with your inner leader, you'll know that although you may seek support for what is most important to you, you'll also look for problems to solve so that you can learn and grow through resolving them. Instead of shrinking from challenges, you'll step up and tackle them, conquer them, master them, and fulfill them.

You become a powerful leader when you can fill the greatest number of voids, answer the most important questions, decipher the most complex puzzles, and solve the greatest mysteries. You understand and embrace the wisdom that you glean from walking the border between support and challenge. As the leader of leaders, you'll become the person who goes into the world striving to fulfill your values while simultaneously providing an invaluable service for humanity. So be open and willing to tackle whatever obstacles come your way.

5. Breaking the Mold

If you're a leader, you're dedicated to the vision in your heart. This is your guiding truth. Your vision embodies what you're really up to, your *raison d'être.* Be willing to follow your master plan even to the point where it breaks through the stagnant or unwise rules of others. Don't allow existing standards or conventions to stop you from pursuing your dream. As I said earlier, I'd rather have the entire world against me than my own soul. Leaders perceive the values of others and can even articulate their inspiring visions in terms of what is most important to those individuals. Visionaries fulfill their purpose by helping others fulfill theirs.

6. Valuing Your Own Time

Another trait of leadership is the ability and willingness to value your own time. Innovators cherish every moment. If you don't set an agenda for your day and follow your high-priority action steps, you'll seldom accomplish all the things you'd hoped to. Balance out your narcissistic desire to do things for yourself with a more selfless desire to solve other people's problems. Doing so helps you refine your goals so that you can continue pursuing your inspired destiny. Break through any momentary stagnations, and keep on tweaking your master plan. Leaders live in the questions, uncovering the answers and solving problems. Be sure to value your time by wisely managing each day in your pursuit of your inspired destiny.

7. Embracing Your Leadership

This concept calls for a more thorough explanation so that you know exactly what I mean regarding this final trait. To embrace your inner leader, summon the courage to be authentic. It doesn't matter what you've been through or what you're currently experiencing. What matters most is that right now, you're making a decision to apply the principles that bring out the leader in you. The moment your decision is made and you start doing what works—honoring your genuine self and your highest values—it's nearly impossible to stop you from fulfilling your purpose.

To influence others in a significant way, you need to be able to look at yourself in front of a mirror and love and respect every aspect of who you are. If you don't love and respect yourself, then why would the world love and value you? If you're unsure about following your dream, then why would someone else follow you? If you aren't inspired to get up in the morning and work toward your goals, then why should someone else be enthusiastic about helping you succeed? If you don't want to be around yourself, then why would anyone else want to be around you?

The outer world reflects what is going on in your inner world. When you value yourself, the people in your life value you. When you're inspired by your destiny, others are, too. When you invest in yourself, other people will invest in you. And when you pay yourself first, other people will pay you first. If you can articulate your vision and purpose in a meaningful way, powerful opportunities will open up around you.

Remember that leaders neither act subordinate to the people around them nor do they inject others' values into their life to become someone they're not. It's vital to embrace who you are and stay true to your highest values. Go out in the world and make a difference through the authentic message that comes from your balanced mind and open heart.

Don't Deny Your Ability to Lead

Give yourself permission to incorporate all seven leadership qualities into your everyday life. Honor the people who inspire you by standing on their shoulders instead of minimizing yourself by feeling inferior to them. You can be a leader on any level, from your community to your nation and beyond, but you must acknowledge and unveil the emerging leader inside. As an inspired leader, I consider every city I visit as another platform where I may share my heart's message. And until my message has reached every country in the world, I haven't fulfilled my life purpose.

Think of it in this way: what else are you going to get up in the morning to do if it's not what you love? A leader does whatever it takes, travels whatever distance, and pays whatever price to pursue his or her inspired destiny.

And here's a bit of parting advice on this topic: you can't fake being inspired or enthusiastic about going after your dreams and providing your service to the world. Gandhi declared that his commitment wasn't to the people, but to the truth. "Truth is my God," he said. If God told him to go left, that's where he'd go, and if others followed, then it would be a blessing, but if they didn't, he understood.

Gandhi led millions of people because of his sincerity to his authentic mission for humanity. Following his example, I'm dedicated to *my* unique mission. I research, write, travel, and speak about Universal Laws as they relate to human behavior every single day. No one has to get me out of bed in the morning to do what I love. I've given more than 400 speeches a year for the past few years, and if I could do more, I would! In fact, one of my goals is to break my own record each year. Don't deny yourself the opportunity to discover your innate leadership skills.

Inspired Insights

- Throughout the ages, there have been leaders who viewed the world from a different vantage point, and these individuals had the courage to speak up about what they saw.

- Genuine leaders are clear on their purpose, vision, and destiny; they have a certainty about themselves in the world. They set goals with integrity, tackle challenges head-on, and are willing to go against current conventions.

- If you don't set the agenda for your day by following your high-priority action steps, you'll seldom (if ever) get as much done as those who do.

- You have a powerful, inspiring leader buried in your heart. Now is the time to let this guiding force out into the world.

Words of Power

Choose at least one of the following affirmations and repeat it to yourself every day for at least the next month (ideally for the next few months). If this seems particularly challenging (or particularly rewarding), make a commitment to repeat it to yourself every day for the rest of your life.

I embrace the duality of life and stay focused on my vision.

I am a powerful and inspiring leader, and I bring my vision to life.

I have the courage to be authentic.

I am inspired by my life mission, and so is the rest of the world.

CHAPTER 20

Getting Your *S* in Gear to Become a Leader

"If your actions inspire others to dream more, learn more,
do more and become more, you are a leader."
— John Quincy Adams

Now that you know the traits of a leader, how exactly do you apply them to your everyday activities? As I was figuring this out for myself, I came up with five *S* words that sum it up. When you incorporate their teachings into your own life, you'll enhance your ability to be the master of your destiny, as well as an inspiring leader to everyone you encounter.

1. Service

The first *S* of leadership is clarifying your unique *service* to the world. To fully embrace the leader within, visualize your service in great detail and be inspired by it. Inspiration is the most powerful leadership tool there is because it calls for action, and it will provide you with the fuel you need to achieve your goals. Your inspiration in life is directly proportional to how vivid your vision is. It's also directly proportional to how clearly you can articulate your purpose statement.

If I asked you to tell me how you'd serve others by doing what you love, and you hesitated in your answer, this would indicate that your vision is unclear and may not inspire you. It's vital to know how your service will fulfill your destiny. Effective leaders know what is truly important to them and what aligns with their highest values. Be sure to follow your inner voice instead of the outer opinions of the world, and stay true to who you are and what you love.

Keep in mind that when you live in alignment with your highest values, you don't require outside motivation to follow through on tasks. You have the power to pursue your ultimate mission when you're inspired about what you do. This inspiration in service will be the driving force for you to achieve your goals. When you're enthusiastic and in touch, in tune and on target with your highest values, for instance, you don't require a lot of sleep. On the other hand, when you're not inspired, you need a lot of sleep to repair the physiological results of the frustration and inner turmoil you experience because you're not doing what you love.

You'll know that you've captured the essence of your inspired service when you well up with tears of gratitude while providing it to people. When whatever you do is genuine, you *feel* it in your heart. It's worth it to take the time to dig deep and find out what you would love to pursue. Remember that it's the inner clarity regarding who you are and what you do that determines your success in realizing your life dream.

2. Specialized Knowledge

Developing *specialized knowledge* in your field is another important aspect of leadership. Gaining expertise in the area where you desire to lead is essential. Spending time on studying and learning what is inspiring to you can have a tremendous impact on whether or not you achieve your goals. So dedicate yourself to developing specialized knowledge in the area of your greatest inspiration, and master it until you know more about it than anybody else (even if that means knowing more about the art of delegation and how to surround yourself with the wisest masters in the various fields you may require).

Did you know that if you read for just 30 minutes a day on a particular subject, in seven years you can be a thought leader in that area? This has been proven, and I've personally achieved this in many fields. Now, if you study for an hour a day, you can reach this expert level in under four years; and if you commit to three hours a day, then in less than two years you'll be on the cutting edge. When you're vastly informed about something you love, you radiate with it.

Here's a personal story on how I went about acquiring specialized knowledge when I was a young man. One day in early November years ago, my mother came into my room and asked me what I'd like to have for my birthday (I was born on Thanksgiving Day).

I said, "Mom, I want the greatest teachings on the face of the earth—the most revered texts that human beings have ever created and known about, from all over the world. I want everything I can get my hands on about the Laws of the Universe."

"Is there anything else you want, son?"

"No, that's all I care about."

"Okay. Let me see what I can do." My mother called her brother, a former professor at MIT who was a physicist and chemist, and asked him if he could recommend something. He ended up sending two giant wooden crates to our house on a flatbed truck! They were deposited on our front yard because they were too large to carry inside. Inspired, I grabbed a crowbar, opened up the massive boxes, and started making piles of book after book. My room was literally filling up with books. I sat there as a recluse, fasting and reading everything I could about the Laws of the Universe. It didn't matter what it was: I was inspired to learn. And the more

I learned, the more inspired I became, and the more others were drawn to me to learn from me.

When you're filling your mind with morsels of wisdom that inspire you, then whatever topic or discipline you're studying tends to be drawn to you like metal to a magnet. This is something I noticed when I was still practicing as a chiropractor. If I went to seminars and learned about back pain, then patients who experienced back pain started making appointments with me. If I learned about headaches, then I'd get calls from patients who were complaining about having headaches. If I learned about cardiovascular disease, then patients with heart problems started showing up in my appointment book—and the list went on. I continually drew into my life whatever topic or symptom I was concentrating on at that moment in time. Once again, remember that your innermost dominant thought becomes your outermost tangible reality.

Any energy or matter that isn't consumed by high-priority actions and thoughts will get consumed by low-priority ones. And if you don't make the effort to consciously fill your day with what feeds your mind, then you'll find that your day becomes filled with uninspiring, insignificant things.

When I was a young boy, my next-door neighbor Mrs. Grubs once told me something very interesting. I was weeding the garden, and she said that if I didn't start planting flowers, I'd be forever pulling weeds. To that end, if you don't focus on what you love every day, then what you don't love will keep on sprouting up in your life. This can be prevented by concentrating and increasing your skills in that area. You'll build your confidence and certainty, which attracts new opportunities. Once you master specialized knowledge, you automatically awaken the powerful, authentic leader within and become the author of your own inspired destiny.

3. Speaking

The third S of leadership is mastering the ability to *speak*. If you can overcome any fear of public speaking, then you automatically move into the top 20 percent of the world's population. Consider what that means: if there are 7 billion people in the world, this means that you're among the top 1.4 billion. You step into this position purely through your ability to stand in front of a group and share what is inside your heart. The majority are afraid to speak up, and they hold themselves back throughout their lives. When you overcome this fear, you're automatically bringing out the leader inside you.

Now if you can speak *and* move your listeners to take action in their own lives, then you're in the top 20 percent of that top 20 percent. And if you can inspire individuals and awaken their authenticity, then you step into the top 20 percent of the previous figure!

When you cause other people to work toward fulfilling their own highest values, they in turn influence others through the human ripple effect. In other words, those whom you inspire go on to inspire others, who inspire others, who inspire others, and so on. When you love what you do and you're aligned with what is most important in your life, you speak freely from your heart. And when you do, you have the power to open the hearts of those who are listening to you, which awakens them to speak from their heart as you have. If you can do this, then you can move in the top 20 percent of the 20 percent of the 20 percent of the 20 percent of the world. Are you still with me? The bottom line is that you become a powerful, influential leader.

With any speaking ability, you're not only clear on your dedicated service for the world, but you also have the ability to talk about what you've learned with an open heart. You'll possess tremendous charisma that draws people to you who want to hear what you have to say. You'll have a voice that touches lives, as well as a steadiness and firmness about who you are. Your magnetism will attract into your life what you think about, visualize, speak about, and dream about the most. When you're doing what you love and loving what you do—and you're inspired while embracing both support and challenge and pleasure and pain—you'll become poised, present, purposeful, and powerful and thousands if not millions will want to be in your inspiring presence.

A person with a mission has a message; and when you discover that message within yourself, your career, relationships, wealth, and life will bloom. When you can't wait to share your message with people, they can't wait to hear it. Speaking and sharing what is buried in your heart is essential in waking up your potential to be a leader.

4. Selling

Another significant aspect of leadership is *selling,* because nothing ever gets done in the world until someone sells something (a product or a message) to someone else. Selling is the ability to communicate what inspires you to others in a way that inspires or somehow moves them. You become a master when you care about people and genuinely love to help them get what they love in life.

When you're selling something that inspires you—and you know in your heart that this is your service to the world—you develop specialized knowledge about it, you speak up and communicate it in a way that other people are served by it, and you demonstrate an incredible power to influence the world.

5. Saving

The fifth and final *S* of leadership is the ability to create financial stability. *Saving* is the willingness to take a portion of everything you earn and first build financial safety cushions, and then invest in the circulating economy as well as your goals. The moment you do, the world around you begins reflecting the world within you. Remember that when you value yourself, the world values you. The very cause that you're dedicated to and investing in will radiate from you, and outside forces will rally around you to help bring your visualizations into reality.

It's possible to achieve your most inspiring outcome when you have that focus and energy on service. Wealth grows and flows where it's appreciated the most. When you make a habit out of saving a portion of everything you earn, you increase the probability of your own financial independence.

Start today by implementing an automatic, electronic monthly withdrawal of at least ten percent of everything you earn, and deposit it into a long-term savings account. Then transfer some of it into an investment account that's designed for growth and preservation until the interest it earns can cover your needs. Utilize the skills you learned earlier in this book to dissolve any feelings of guilt that you may have about amassing wealth so that you can remove any blocks that could stop you from building great resources for yourself, your inspired social service, and your destiny.

Think of it in this way: If you have no savings (zero dollars), then you hang out with "zeroaires." If you have $10 saved, then you hang out with "tenaires." If you have $100 saved, then you hang out with "hundredaires." If you have $1,000,000 saved, then you hang out with millionaires, and on it goes. So every time you begin to save and invest—you pay yourself first because you value yourself—you get more than just compound interest. You get to associate with wealthy, service-focused people; incubate ideas; and be presented with opportunities that can increase your wealth as well as help you do what you love.

There is zero risk in saving money. The worst thing that could happen is that if a very large bill comes along, you'll have to cash out your savings. There is no risk in trying to save, but there is a risk in not trying because you'll eventually burn yourself out by not rewarding yourself for your inspired service. *You* are the most important person in *your* life, and nobody gets up in the morning to dedicate his or her life to you. You're it!

Integrate and Apply the Five S's of Leadership to Your Life

When you integrate and apply the five S's of leadership into your life, you'll notice significant changes in the way you appreciate yourself and the way other people interact with you. The more you enhance your authentic sense of leadership within, the more the people around you, as well as the rest of the world, will acknowledge you as a leader. Whether you'd like to be a leader in music, writing, sports, fashion, or environmentalism (or whatever area you're drawn to), you have what it takes to be an inspiring leader in your chosen field.

Inspired Insights

- The five S's of leadership are service, specialized knowledge, speaking, selling, and saving.

- Set an inspiring example for others by sharing your message and uncovering your natural leadership skills.

- The more you enhance your authentic sense of leadership, the more that people around you (as well as the rest of the world) will acknowledge you as a master in your field.

- Applying the five aspects of leadership will powerfully assist you in fulfilling your inspired destiny.

Words of Power

Choose at least one of the following affirmations and repeat it to yourself every day for at least the next month (ideally for the next few months). If this seems particularly challenging (or particularly rewarding), make a commitment to repeat it to yourself every day for the rest of your life.

I know my inspired service for humanity.

I invest time into gaining specialized knowledge in the fields I love.

I share my message with everyone I meet.

I am a dedicated, inspired leader of others.

CHAPTER 21

The Ripple Effect

"Never doubt that a small group of thoughtful, committed citizens can change the world. Indeed, it is the only thing that ever has."
— **Margaret Mead**

People often underestimate the power they have as individuals to make a significant impact on the world. Yet when you're acting on your purpose, it's highly likely that you're going to feel a strong desire to continue spreading your message—serving and engaging people through your vision—until you've possibly reached every human being on Earth. You might have an immediate group of supporters who are moved by your inspired purpose. And after realizing the powerful difference you've made in the lives of these individuals, you'll probably desire to go on and make an even bigger impact to find out who else your product, service, or idea can benefit or serve.

To make the greatest possible impact, you'll eventually keep expanding your mission from your immediate circle of influence to the entire planet. It will be wise for you to observe and keep track of how everything you do affects people and the ways in which you enhance their quality of life—all through doing what you love, loving what you do, and getting financially rewarded to do it. The more your service grows, the more individuals you reach and inspire, then the more your mind and heart will open.

I once consulted with a builder in Denver, Colorado, who was responsible for hundreds of new homes throughout the United States. Together, we explored the impact that his company had on the world. We went through all of the different levels, from the roots of construction to the end results, until we were thinking about the men and women in other countries who were creating and providing the resources that he required for his projects. We talked about the metal, stone, and other materials he used, and how these things had been extracted and refined until they were suitable for his needs. His vocation was putting lots of people on the other side of the world into business by purchasing, for example, slate from one area of the planet or marble and granite from other areas.

We then took it a step further and thought of the children who were able to go to school because of the jobs he was indirectly supplying to their parents. We thought of the teachers who had jobs because their students' parents also had jobs. We continued discussing this until he became momentarily silent, and then simply said, "Wow." He was clearly overwhelmed by the enormity of the vision he had just seen and how what he did every day impacted countless people.

How do you make a difference that touches the lives of thousands or even millions of people around the world? When you realize that you have a higher purpose—and you can see the big picture—you add force to your vision and fuel to your inspiration.

Learning the Ripple Effect

My father owned and operated a high-end, prestigious plumbing company in Houston. When I was a youngster, probably about five or six years old, he was ready to put me to work. That was okay with me; I considered becoming a plumber myself at that age and was always eager to watch a master tradesman practice his trade. One day, my dad said to me, "I want you to go on a job with Jesse Carter and be his helper. You'll learn a lot."

Jesse, who was the ditchdigger, was in his 30s and game to work with a young boy. We drove to the customer's home and began working in the yard where we were going to install a new water line that ran from the street water main to the house. Jesse used a T-bar to locate anything that was underneath the surface—such as roots, rocks, and other obstructions—and also to determine the grade in the ground. I watched him as he traced the route where he was going to dig the ditch.

He gave me jobs to do, like watering down the ground in certain areas and checking the depth so that he could work with softened earth instead of rocky, clumpy soil. Then he and I laid out some tar paper and cardboard along the side of the route so that we wouldn't lose any dirt on the grass beside the ditch. He then tested to make sure the water had reached a certain depth so he could dig quickly and efficiently. In that moment, I realized what a careful worker Jesse was, doing everything possible to make a proper ditch, even ensuring that no grass, trees, roots, plants, or flowers were disturbed in the process. He then showed me the next steps: carefully placing the sod and fill to the side, putting the pipe in perfectly graded so that no rust or stains would appear as well as using the fewest possible joints. After the pipe was inserted to his satisfaction, we refilled the dirt, removed the tar paper and cardboard, and cleaned up the yard.

Jesse explained to me that the whole procedure was to minimize the possibility of damage that might occur to the pipe in the next 20 to 30 years. This man was so efficient and effective at digging ditches that customers would often call my father when they got home from work and ask why he didn't send out people to do the job. No one would believe that Jesse had dug a large ditch in their yard earlier in the day!

Now, the reason why my father wanted me to accompany Jesse on the job was because he was a master. He was a genius at what he did. Jesse believed that the world depended on him, because no family could function without water, and his job was to safely connect people to the source. As he told me, "My job is to bring the community to the people and the people to the community. My work is vital."

Jesse understood the ripple effect. He saw his supposedly insignificant, everyday job in terms of how it impacted the world. He could see how doing his job with integrity and mastery would set the stage for higher standards. He was responsible for producing higher-quality water, ensuring that it was clean with no rust or chemicals that shouldn't be there naturally. He was thinking way outside the box, and his work was an inspiration. Jesse was just as inspired about digging a ditch as he was about raising his children and providing for his family.

You just never know where your inspired destiny might take you once you acknowledge your own unique ripple effect.

Exercise: Get Inspired!

Recognize Your Ripple Effect

1. Think about any action that you've taken. (For example, "I gave a book to a friend.")

2. Write down anyone who was moved or somehow affected by what you did. (For example, "My friend was deeply inspired by the book's message and passed the book on to her mother.")

3. In what ways did your action cause the individuals who were inspired to inspire additional people? (For example, "My friend's mom took the book to one of her club meetings and shared its message with *her* friends.")

4. How did that act continue to touch even more people? (For example, "The people who were in the book club were inspired and shared the message with *their* family members.")

5. Continue on the same path: how did that act continue spiraling out to inspire more and more people? (For example, "The spouse of one of the book club members was a teacher who brought the book into her classroom and shared the message with her students.")

Keep asking and answering these questions until you can see how monumental the effect of one simple action can be in creating an endless spiral that touches countless individuals. Experience the human ripple effect and the ways in which the people you influence go on to influence others, who influence others, and on and on it goes infinitely.

There's no need to doubt the power that you have to make a global impact. I once completed this exercise with an eight-year-old boy who was convinced that he didn't have any kind of profound effect. When I asked him if he'd ever bought anything, he told me that just the day before, his mom had sent him to the store to buy a bar of soap.

"Really? That's huge! Who sold you the soap?" He told me there was a woman working the cash register, who was the owner of the small convenience store in his neighborhood. So we talked about how that woman probably had a family, how she must buy her soap from a distributor, and how that distributor probably had a family, too. And what about the distributor's employer? That company needed people like the distributor to operate, and how many other employees depended on that company for their livelihood? But all that talk about business wasn't really getting through to the youngster.

I asked him if he knew how soap was made, and he shook his head.

"Well, there are a lot of ingredients, like oils, herbs, spices, and perfumes. People all over the world make these things that, when combined, form a single bar of soap."

"So, me buying one bar of soap helps people all over the world?"

"Yes! And you know how that bar of soap is wrapped in paper?"

He was catching on and quickly replied, "Somebody wrote what is on the paper, and somebody came up with the name for the soap! Another person picked the color of the paper, and someone else made the paper!"

"You've got it. In addition, somebody arranged for the transport of the paper from where it was made to where the soap was packaged, and for the transport of the soap from the factory to the packaging plant, too."

"Hey, what about the people who are in the commercials for the soap on TV, and the people who make up those commercials, and the people who write the rules for what you can put in a commercial, and the people who . . . ?" Now he was really getting it. We talked about that bar of soap for close to an hour.

It's important to know that everything you do—and particularly, whatever you do within your life's purpose—impacts people around you in ways that will leave you awestruck when you become aware of it. You just have to take the time to look.

How You Can Set an Example for the World

By honoring your unique hierarchy of values and setting goals that are aligned with your highest values, you have the potential to touch people around the world just by living your inspired destiny. You can work at the bottom of a company or organization and still have the greatest impact on others, directly and indirectly, through your everyday actions. Heed the yearning inside of you to do something amazing. When you put your whole heart into what you do and acknowledge the impact you have, you automatically increase the probability of getting where you'd love to be in life.

I often say that when you make yourself as indispensable as possible, you become indispensable to the world, and the world demands your service. Consistently overdelivering on what is expected of you will make it almost impossible for you to ever be out of a job. Become inspired, link everything you do to your highest values, embrace your purpose, and let that influence rub off on everything you touch. Set an example for others by pursuing a meaningful, fulfilling existence; and everyone around you will become inspired by your presence.

When you fully recognize and acknowledge the effect you have on the lives of others, your drive to achieve your goals will increase, you'll become more prosperous, and you'll want to contribute even more so that you leave an immortal legacy. Stop and reflect on the ways you impact the world, and take your purpose sky-high in fulfilling your inspired destiny.

Inspired Insights

- Most people underestimate the power they have to make a significant global impact just by living their inspired destiny.

- Take the time to see how your everyday actions affect others across the world.

- Keep asking yourself, *How does this action touch the world?* until you can truly comprehend how everything you do has a profound effect upon your surroundings (and beyond).

- Set an example for others on what it means to live a fulfilling life, and those around you will automatically be inspired by your powerful, loving presence.

- Examine the part that you play in the human ripple effect.

Words of Power

Choose at least one of the following affirmations and repeat it to yourself every day for at least the next month (ideally for the next few months). If this seems particularly challenging (or particularly rewarding), make a commitment to repeat it to yourself every day for the rest of your life.

Every action I take has a monumental influence on the lives of others.

I touch the entire world by fulfilling my inspired destiny.

I am destined to make a global impact and leave an immortal legacy.

The greater an impact I make, the more inspired I am to pursue all of my goals.

CONCLUSION

You are here to live purposefully . . . to uncover your magnificent life . . . to make an extraordinary difference in the world . . . and to leave an immortal legacy.

Let nothing on the face of the earth stop you from
fulfilling your inspired destiny.
Give yourself permission to shine!

ACKNOWLEDGMENTS

I would love to give special thanks to several people who made this book possible.

First, to Emily Gowor for assisting me in organizing the transcripts from my live Young Adults Inspired Destiny events and other seminars, interviews, and published articles; as well as composing a series of initial drafts until the primary working manuscript could emerge into tangible reality. Thank you for being an inspired word artist and young visionary. Without your talents, this book would not have made it to the form it is today.

To Karen Risch for adding her magic touch to this manuscript so that my teachings could see the light of day. Thank you for cleaning up the grammar, polishing the creative expression, and helping me give birth to another book baby.

I would love to give special thanks to Clarissa Judd for her intense dedication to introducing the Demartini Institute—along with its principles, methodologies, teaching programs, and humanitarian services—to people of all ages and sectors of society across the world; for envisioning and initiating the first Young Adults Inspired Destiny program in South Africa; for her special assistance in organizing the initial workbook for this program; and finally, for transcribing, collating, and editing the original and final manuscripts of the book you're now holding in your hands.

To Steve Momen, Edwin Hawthorn, and Taddy Blecher for their dedication to education in South Africa and for their assistance in getting the ball rolling.

To Carla Bester and Minalli Patel for patiently sitting for hours and transcribing all the audio recordings from the education talks and Young Adults Inspired Destiny programs.

To the many young men and women I've been fortunate enough to have in attendance at my Young Adults Inspired Destiny programs in South Africa. Without their smiling, shining faces; challenged beginnings; inspired dreams; and studious attendance; this book would not have been conceived.

To all of the team players at Hay House for their continued expertise and support in taking manuscripts and turning them into books that are able to be distributed and sold in many languages and countries throughout the world.

ABOUT THE AUTHOR

Dr. John F. Demartini is a human behavioral specialist, educator, internationally published author, and sought-after authority on maximizing human awareness and potential. The founder of the Demartini Institute, he is one of the more brilliant minds alive today. Encompassing a broad scope of knowledge in more than 275 different disciplines, including physics, philosophy, theology, metaphysics, psychology, astronomy, mathematics, neurology, and physiology, Dr. Demartini's work on human behavior is revolutionary. He has appeared in numerous international magazines and newspapers, as well as interviews on more than 4,000 radio and television talk shows worldwide.

Developing a powerful methodology in personal and professional transformation known as The Demartini Method®—the Tool with 1,000 Uses for Mastering Life, Dr. Demartini now travels full-time throughout the world sharing his knowledge and insights on human behavior. He has educated millions of people on how to break through whatever is holding them back, helping them empower themselves and achieve their dreams.

For more information on Dr. Demartini or to attend one of his seminars (including Young Adults Inspired Destiny or The Breakthrough Experience®), please contact:

The Demartini Institute
2800 Post Oak Blvd., Suite 5250
Houston, TX 77056
Toll-free: (888) 336-2784 • *Phone:* (713) 850-1234
Fax: (713) 850-9239
E-mail: **info@drdemartini.com**
Website: **www.drdemartini.com**

Hay House Titles of Related Interest

YOU CAN HEAL YOUR LIFE, *the movie,*
starring Louise Hay & Friends
(available as a 1-DVD program and an expanded 2-DVD set)
Watch the trailer at: **www.LouiseHayMovie.com**

THE SHIFT, *the movie,*
starring Dr. Wayne W. Dyer
(available as a 1-DVD program and an expanded 2-DVD set)
Watch the trailer at: **www.DyerMovie.com**

THE EVEREST PRINCIPLE: How to Achieve the Summit of Your Life,
by Stephen C. Brewer, M.D., and Peggy Holt Wagner, M.S., L.P.C.

**EXCUSES BEGONE! How to Change Lifelong,
Self-Defeating Thinking Habits,** by Dr. Wayne W. Dyer

**MODERN-DAY MIRACLES: Miraculous Moments and Extraordinary
Stories from People All Over the World Whose Lives Have
Been Touched by Louise Hay,** by Louise Hay & Friends

**THE POWER OF INFINITE LOVE & GRATITUDE: An Evolutionary
Journey to Awakening Your Spirit,** by Darren R. Weissman

**SIMPLY . . . EMPOWERED! Discover How to CREATE and SUSTAIN
Success in Every Area of Your Life,** by Crystal Andrus

**SOUL COACHING: 28 Days to Discovering
Your Authentic Self,** by Denise Linn

**THE WON THING: The "One" Secret to a
Totally Fulfilling Life,** by Peggy McColl

All of the above are available at your local bookstore,
or may be ordered by contacting Hay House (see next page).

We hope you enjoyed this Hay House book. If you'd like to receive our online catalog featuring additional information on Hay House books and products, or if you'd like to find out more about the Hay Foundation, please contact:

Hay House, Inc., P.O. Box 5100, Carlsbad, CA 92018-5100
(760) 431-7695 or **(800) 654-5126**
(760) 431-6948 (fax) or **(800) 650-5115 (fax)**
www.hayhouse.com® • **www.hayfoundation.org**

Published and distributed in Australia by: Hay House Australia Pty. Ltd., 18/36 Ralph St., Alexandria NSW 2015 • *Phone:* 612-9669-4299 *Fax:* 612-9669-4144 • www.hayhouse.com.au

Published and distributed in the United Kingdom by: Hay House UK, Ltd., Astley House, 33 Notting Hill Gate, London W11 3JQ • *Phone:* 44-20-3675-2450 • *Fax:* 44-20-3675-2451 • www.hayhouse.co.uk

Published and distributed in the Republic of South Africa by: Hay House SA (Pty), Ltd., P.O. Box 990, Witkoppen 2068 info@hayhouse.co.za • www.hayhouse.co.za

Published in India by: Hay House Publishers India, Muskaan Complex, Plot No. 3, B-2, Vasant Kunj, New Delhi 110 070 • *Phone:* 91-11-4176-1620 • *Fax:* 91-11-4176-1630 • www.hayhouse.co.in

Distributed in Canada by: Raincoast Books, 2440 Viking Way, Richmond, B.C. V6V 1N2 • *Phone:* 1-800-663-5714 *Fax:* 1-800-565-3770 • www.raincoast.com

Take Your Soul on a Vacation

Visit **www.HealYourLife.com®** to regroup, recharge, and reconnect with your own magnificence. Featuring blogs, mind-body-spirit news, and life-changing wisdom from Louise Hay and friends.

Visit **www.HealYourLife.com** today!

Printed in the United States
By Bookmasters